Contents

Introduction ☆☆☆☆☆☆☆☆☆☆☆☆☆☆☆☆☆☆☆☆☆☆☆☆☆☆

Cast Your Vote is a flexible resource that can be used during an election year or at any time to extend social studies, government, and civics lessons. It is divided into five sections:

(1) background information on voting and various levels of government in the United States;

(2) elected positions leadership at the federal, state, and local levels;

(3) the election process;

(4) projects dealing with conducting a class election and following an actual election; and

(5) background resources.

Throughout the book you will find a Presidential Trivia feature that highlights an interesting historical fact about a president, candidates for office, or other political information. You may use these items to create a trivia game for your students, or have the students create a game on their own.

Activities include those that can be done independently and those that require working with partners or in groups. All topics benefit from discussion. The two project sections, Conduct an Election and Follow an Election, require some organizational management and cooperation with the community and/or the school. You can alter these projects as you see fit to match your community's circumstances. For instance, instead of voting for a liaison with the local police, students could vote on how to address another problem in the community. Draw from your students' interests to make the election lively and engaging. You could limit the activity to one area of the community or expand it to encompass a broader area. The more involved students become in the election process at this age, the better prepared they will be to accept the responsibilities of true citizens of a democracy.

Correlation to Standards ☆☆☆☆☆☆☆☆☆☆☆☆☆☆☆☆☆☆

Structure of Government
- Describe how the Constitution is designed to limit central government and create a separation of powers.
- Differentiate the roles and powers of the three branches of the federal government.
- Explain the electoral process.
- Explain how a candidate can be elected president without receiving a majority of the popular vote (Electoral College system).
- Analyze the forms, structure, powers, and roles of local governments.

Functions of Government
- Analyze the functions of government as defined in the Preamble to the Constitution.
- Describe the responsibilities of state and local governments.
- Identify the government's role in reforms (e.g., women's suffrage, civil rights).
- Describe forms of direct democracy: initiative, referendum, recall process.
- Compare the roles and relationships of different levels of government.

Rights, Responsibilities, and Roles of Citizenship
- Describe the importance of citizens being actively involved in the democratic process (e.g., voting, campaigning, analyzing issues, evaluating candidates, petitioning public officials).
- Describe the role and influence of political parties, interest groups, and mass media.

Name _____   Date _____

Assessment

Darken the letter of the correct answer.

1. Which of the following is NOT one branch of the national government?
   Ⓐ federal
   Ⓑ executive
   Ⓒ legislative
   Ⓓ judicial

2. All of the following government officials are elected by the voters EXCEPT
   Ⓐ a mayor.
   Ⓑ a senator.
   Ⓒ a Supreme Court justice.
   Ⓓ a representative.

3. What is the minimum legal voting age in the United States?
   Ⓐ 16
   Ⓑ 18
   Ⓒ 21
   Ⓓ 25

4. Which best describes the government of the United States?
   Ⓐ a democracy
   Ⓑ a dictatorship
   Ⓒ a monarchy
   Ⓓ a republic

5. When you vote for president on Election Day in November, for whom have you actually cast your vote?
   Ⓐ the president
   Ⓑ the vice president
   Ⓒ delegates who will vote for the president
   Ⓓ electors who will vote for the president

6. The number of electoral votes allotted to each state is determined by the state's
   Ⓐ geographical size.
   Ⓑ population.
   Ⓒ order of entry into the United States.
   Ⓓ economy.

7. Which of these states holds the earliest presidential primary election in the nation?
   Ⓐ Massachusetts
   Ⓑ New York
   Ⓒ New Hampshire
   Ⓓ Washington

8. How many voting members are there in the U.S. Senate?
   Ⓐ 9
   Ⓑ 50
   Ⓒ 100
   Ⓓ 435

9. Which of the following has always been elected by direct popular vote?
   Ⓐ president
   Ⓑ vice president
   Ⓒ senator
   Ⓓ representative

10. Which of the following can best help you if you support a smoking ban in your city?
   Ⓐ your governor
   Ⓑ your mayor
   Ⓒ your city council representative
   Ⓓ your state senator

Assessment
Cast Your Vote HS, SV 9781419036378

Assessment, page 2

11. Citizens can play a direct role in their state government through all of the following means EXCEPT
   Ⓐ a veto.
   Ⓑ an initiative.
   Ⓒ a referendum.
   Ⓓ a recall.

12. The Nineteenth Amendment gave the right to vote to
   Ⓐ 18-year-olds.
   Ⓑ African Americans.
   Ⓒ women.
   Ⓓ Native Americans.

13. Which of the following is responsible for running national elections?
   Ⓐ the national government
   Ⓑ the state
   Ⓒ the county
   Ⓓ the city

14. Which word describes a government in which authority is shared between the national and state governments?
   Ⓐ democratic
   Ⓑ federal
   Ⓒ republican
   Ⓓ socialist

15. The laws of the United States are set down in a document called
   Ⓐ the Declaration of Independence.
   Ⓑ the Constitution.
   Ⓒ the Oath of Office.
   Ⓓ the Code of Laws.

16. The plan of action of a political party is called its
   Ⓐ platform.
   Ⓑ budget.
   Ⓒ document.
   Ⓓ ballot.

17. What are held before many elections to help voters learn the differences between the candidates on important issues?
   Ⓐ conventions
   Ⓑ debates
   Ⓒ polls
   Ⓓ referendums

18. A presidential candidate for each party is chosen at the party's
   Ⓐ primary election.
   Ⓑ voting booth.
   Ⓒ state convention.
   Ⓓ national convention.

19. The power of each branch of government is limited through
   Ⓐ Congress.
   Ⓑ checks and balances.
   Ⓒ amendments.
   Ⓓ states' rights.

20. Which branch of government decides whether the actions of the president or the laws of Congress are constitutional?
   Ⓐ legislative
   Ⓑ executive
   Ⓒ judicial
   Ⓓ federal

Name _____ Date _____

Voting

The Right to Vote

A **vote** is the statement of a choice. If someone asks "Should we have chicken or fish for dinner?" and you answer "Fish," you have just cast your vote.

The right to vote means that you can express your opinion and others will respect it. It means that when you say "I want fish for dinner" or "I want that person to be president," your vote is counted equally with everyone else's. This is an important principle of democratic government.

Today, all U.S. citizens age 18 and older, except those convicted of certain crimes, have the right to vote. This has not always been the case. Different categories of Americans have had to fight for this right throughout history. The time line below shows you how the **franchise** has been gradually extended.

1789	The Constitution is ratified, and white male citizens age 21 and older have the right to vote. This is less than 40 percent of all adults.
1868, 1870	The Fourteenth and Fifteenth **Amendments** grant African American men age 21 and older the right to vote.
1920	The Nineteenth Amendment guarantees women age 21 and older the right to vote. Women had begun to fight for **suffrage** in large numbers in the 1880s. Four states had granted women the right to vote before the Nineteenth Amendment was passed.
1924	Native Americans are granted full citizenship, including the right to vote.
1964	The Twenty-fourth Amendment declares that **poll taxes** are illegal. A poll tax is a charge for voting. Southern states established poll taxes after the Civil War. Most former slaves were too poor to afford the tax and were thus prevented from voting. The Twenty-fourth Amendment enabled thousands more African Americans to vote.
1971	The Twenty-sixth Amendment lowers the voting age from 21 to 18. Many young people had protested the Vietnam War. They were angry at being drafted into the armed forces. They argued that if they were old enough to die for their country, they were old enough to vote for the leaders who sent them to war.

Voting, continued

The Privilege of Voting

Voting is not only a right, but a privilege. A person who can vote is lucky to have the chance to do so. The privilege of voting should be taken seriously. Your vote will help determine who will run the government of your town, your state, and your country.

Throughout most of the world's history, people have not had this privilege. One family ruled a nation until another family fought the rulers and took over their power. This often happened on the battlefield. The people could decide which side to fight for in battle, but once the government was in place, they had no say about how it was run or who would be the head of the government. Even in societies that had some form of representative government, only a small part of the population could vote.

Today, many nations of the world have some form of representative government. In most of these places, people have the right and privilege of voting. The United States is rare among nations because it was founded on this privilege.

Voting does mean that you have to make some effort. It is up to the voter to follow the news, listen to the candidates during an election, and decide which one would best represent him or her. Informed voters should know what the important issues are and should have a clear opinion about those issues.

Adults who decide not to vote offer many reasons. They complain that things never change; they object to candidates who attack one another; they believe all politicians are dishonest and corrupt; they dislike all of the candidates; and so on. Sometimes people simply do not want to take the trouble to go to the polling place and stand in line to cast their vote. This is a choice every person must make.

PRESIDENTIAL TRIVIA

SEAL OF THE PRESIDENT OF THE UNITED STATES

ZACHARY TAYLOR (1784–1850)

General Zachary Taylor was elected president in 1848. Taylor was a hero of the Mexican-American War. However, he had never voted in an election until he ran for president.

Things to Do:

☑ *Buy Stamps*

☑ *Do Laundry*

☐ *VOTE!*

Citizenship Starts at Home . . .
Take Your Child to Vote!

Name _____ Date _____

Convince a Friend to Vote

Read the introduction. Then follow the steps below.

Introduction

Every election year, all U.S. citizens age 18 and over (except those convicted of certain crimes) have the right to cast their votes. However, there is no law forcing them to vote—and many do not vote. In most presidential election years since 1928, the voter turnout has been between 50 percent and 60 percent of the adult population.

In order to vote, you must register. This is easy to do no matter where you live. Applications are available in places like public libraries and post offices. You can also register online or when you have your driver's license renewed. Even though it is an easy process, many people do not register. In 2000, about 50 million adults did not register to vote.

Choose a partner. Then complete the activity.

You and your partner are going to role-play a conversation. The first person has decided not to vote in a national election. The second person tries to convince the first to cast his or her vote.

Prepare for the conversation individually. Read the lesson on voting. Talk to your parents, your brothers and sisters who are old enough to vote, or to other adults you know well. Ask them why they have voted or refused to vote. Make notes in the space below.

Once you and your partner feel prepared, decide which partner will be on which side of the argument. Then role-play your conversation. Limit yourselves to ten minutes.

Finally, switch roles and repeat the activity. See how well each of you can defend the reasoning of the opposite side.

Reasons That People Should Vote	Reasons That People Do Not Vote

Cast Your Vote HS, SV 9781419036378

Elections

An **election** is a formal event in which people cast their votes for **candidates** for office. The election of officers for a local garden club is a small-scale event. The elections for state and national government officials are on a much larger scale. An election can also be held to determine matters such as designating money to be spent for roads, libraries, and other community resources.

In the United States, the individual states are responsible for running elections. This is true whether the elections are local, national, or a combination of the two. All the different state systems have a great deal in common, but no two states follow exactly the same set of rules.

Election Day in the United States is always on the day after the first Monday in November. Candidates elected on that day take office the following January. This allows time for an orderly transfer of power.

Polls are generally open from 6:00 A.M. or 7:00 A.M. to 7:00 P.M. or 8:00 P.M., so that people can conveniently vote without having to miss school or work.

Because of the difference in time zones across the country, polls on the East Coast open three hours before those on the West Coast and close three hours earlier. This means that races in Eastern states can be decided while people on the West Coast are still voting.

Some people vote electronically. Others fill out paper ballots. Either way, you are always guaranteed privacy in the polling place. The **secret ballot** is an important principle of democracy. No one is allowed to know who cast a vote for which candidate. This means that no one can be attacked for making a particular choice, and no one can be pressured into voting for anyone.

Votes are counted as quickly as possible. Each **precinct** reports vote totals throughout the day to a central headquarters. If the polls close at 8:00 P.M., it's often possible to predict a clear winner by 9:00 P.M. However, many races are so close that the outcome cannot be determined until the following morning.

PRESIDENTIAL TRIVIA

GERALD FORD (1913–2006)

Gerald Ford became president in 1975 without ever being elected. This is how it happened. In 1973, Vice President Spiro Agnew resigned when he was caught accepting bribes. President Richard Nixon appointed Congressman Ford to replace him as vice president. Ford became president himself in 1974 when Nixon resigned.

Name _____ Date _____

Organize an Election

Work together with a small group of classmates to organize and hold an election. Follow these steps:

1. Find some aspect of life at your school that you want to change. Here are some ideas to consider, just to get you started. They are in the form of questions to which students can vote Yes or No.

   - Should everyone have to pass a basic swimming test in order to graduate?
   - Should all students have to take two years of a foreign language to graduate?
   - Should students be able to get course credit for community service or part-time work outside of school?
   - Should all smoking areas be eliminated from the school building?

2. Once your group has chosen an issue, set a date for the election. It should be between one and two weeks after the day you decide your issue.

3. Work together to get classmates interested in voting. Divide the following tasks among the members of your group:

   - getting permission from school officials to conduct your election
   - making speeches to classes or other school gatherings
   - making and displaying posters and flyers urging people to vote on the issue
   - making sure everyone knows when the election will be held

4. During the campaign, you will also have to plan the actual election. Here is a list of tasks:

   - designing a ballot and making enough copies for all voters
   - choosing a place in the school building where students can come to cast their votes
   - counting the votes at the end of the day

5. Once the votes are counted, you will know if the student body as a whole wants the change your group discussed. If it does want the change, think about what your next step should be to bring that change about. Here are some things you might consider:

   - posting the results in the school
   - giving an interview to the school newspaper
   - asking for a meeting with your teacher and other school officials and discussing ways in which the school can make the change you want to see

Government

The word *government* is based on a Latin verb that means "to direct and control." A government is the system by which people are ruled.

You can find systems of government in any group of people who have agreed on a set of rules by which the group will be run. You can find governments in worker's unions, in social clubs, and in schools.

National governments have two main purposes:

- to make and enforce reasonable laws
- to provide necessary services to the people

Rules and Laws

People in most societies can agree on certain sets of rules to live by. It is up to the government to write down those laws and to see that they are not broken. If laws are broken, it is up to the government to punish the lawbreakers.

The laws of the United States are written down in a document called the Constitution. Congress has **amended** the Constitution 27 times since 1789, adding new laws and changing old ones as needed.

Services

Government services include many things you may have always taken for granted. The government provides armed forces that protect the people in times of war. The government builds highways, funds mass transit and the public school system, and provides the postal service. The government also provides health care and old-age pensions.

Not all governments provide the same services to their citizens. In the United States, politicians have generally held two opposing views about government services. Some argue that the government should provide more social services. Others argue that this is not the government's job and that people must provide for themselves. The United States government has provided more or fewer services, depending on the beliefs of the officials in power at any given time.

During the Great Depression of the 1930s, millions of people were out of work. The New Deal under President Franklin D. Roosevelt created programs and projects that provided jobs for these people. During the late 1960s, President Lyndon Johnson's Great Society funded important educational programs such as Head Start.

PRESIDENTIAL TRIVIA

LYNDON B. JOHNSON (1908–1973)

Lyndon Johnson was the thirty-sixth president of the United States. He grew up in a small rural community in central Texas. After he graduated from college, he taught public school in Houston, Texas. There he saw firsthand the effects of poverty on children and their ability to perform in school. This experience was the basis for his "Great Society" and his desire to help young children through the Head Start program.

Government, continued

Throughout history, the nations of the world have had a great variety of different types of government.

Democracy

In a **democracy**, the people rule themselves. This has never been possible except in very small nations. Certain city-states in ancient Greece were democracies. Male citizens took turns in positions of authority and met in groups to decide laws.

Republic

The citizens of a republic elect representatives who make and carry out the laws. The earliest republic in history was two thousand years ago in ancient Rome. The United States is a republic. Some of its institutions, such as the Senate, are specifically modeled on the Roman government.

Hereditary Monarchy

A **monarch** is a member of a ruling family. When the reigning monarch dies, a member of the same family (usually a son or daughter) takes over. Monarchs in history include emperors, pharaohs, czars, kings, and queens.

An **absolute monarch** has total power. The monarch's word is law and cannot be questioned. France was an absolute monarchy until the time of the French Revolution in the late 1700s. The czars of Russia were absolute monarchs.

A **constitutional monarch** is a head of state who does not have total authority. Great Britain is an example of a constitutional monarchy. The Queen of England is the head of state, but the head of the government is the prime minister.

Dictatorship

A **dictator** is a special type of absolute monarch. A dictator did not inherit power. He seized it, usually with the help of the military. Once a dictator is in power, his decisions cannot be questioned by anyone. Elections may sometimes be held in dictatorships, but they do not allow voters any meaningful choices. Examples of dictators in history include Adolf Hitler of Germany in the 1930s and 1940s and Fidel Castro, who has ruled Cuba since the 1950s.

Adolf Hitler

Name _____ Date _____

Governments of the World

☆☆☆☆☆☆☆☆☆☆☆☆☆☆☆☆☆☆☆☆☆☆☆☆☆☆☆☆☆☆☆

Complete the following activity.

Research the current government in one nation of the world other than the United States. First, choose the nation you would like to study. Then complete the information.

1. Nation: _____

2. Describe the type of government in this nation. _____
_____

3. Who is the leader of the government? _____

4. What is his or her official title? _____

5. How is the leader chosen? _____
_____

6. How long can the leader hold office? _____

7. Who are the other important officials in the government? _____
_____
_____

8. What rights and freedoms do the people of this nation enjoy in their relationship to the government?
_____
_____
_____
_____

9. Does this nation hold free elections? If so, how often? _____
_____

10. Draw a time line or write a short paragraph tracing the history of this nation's government, noting the important changes it has gone through. Use a separate sheet of paper.

(For example, the United States was originally individual colonies of a constitutional monarchy, Great Britain. From 1789 to the present, the United States has been a republic.)

Name _____ Date _____

The Federal Government

Many people refer to the United States as a democracy. In fact, it is a republic. This means that the citizens elect representatives who make and carry out the laws.

Three Branches of Government

The national government has three branches: the **legislative,** the **executive,** and the **judicial.** U.S. citizens vote for members of the first two branches only. The Constitution divides power among the three branches so that no branch of the federal government becomes too powerful. This is called the **separation of powers.**

The legislative branch makes the laws. The executive branch carries out the laws. The judicial branch determines whether the laws are **constitutional.** The judicial branch can overturn laws that are unconstitutional.

The citizens can be referred to as the fourth branch of the government. They must obey the laws, but they have the power to vote leaders out of office.

The legislative branch of the government is called **Congress.** Congress is a **bicameral,** or two-chambered, legislature. The upper house of Congress is called the Senate, and the lower house is called the House of Representatives. Both senators and representatives are directly elected by the people.

The most important responsibility of Congress is to make the laws. Individual senators and representatives propose laws to the Congress. Members then debate these bills and make changes to them. Once both houses of Congress are agreed on a bill, it goes to the president for approval. When the president signs the bill, it becomes a law. If he refuses to sign the bill, a two-thirds majority of Congress can **override** his **veto.**

The executive branch of the government is the **presidency.** The president and vice president of the United States are elected indirectly by the people. The president is the head of state. He (or she) represents the United States in meetings with other world leaders. The president negotiates peace treaties, trade agreements, and other aspects of international relations. The president also speaks directly to the press and the citizens, informing them of important decisions and answering questions.

The judicial branch of the government is the **Supreme Court** of the United States. Supreme Court justices are appointed by the president and must then be confirmed by the Senate. Citizens may vote for judges in their local courts, but they do not have any say in who will sit on the Supreme Court.

PRESIDENTIAL TRIVIA

JAMES MADISON (1751–1836)

James Madison of Virginia played a central role in the writing and ratification of the Constitution. Madison and two others wrote an important series of essays called *The Federalist Papers* to persuade Americans to support the Constitution. Madison is known to history as the Father of the Constitution. He served as president from 1809 to 1817.

The Federal Government, continued

Checks and Balances

The key feature of the U.S. government is the **checks and balances** built into it. Each of the three branches of government can check the power of the other two. This means that no one branch can acquire too much power.

This chart shows the powers that each branch of the federal government has over the other two.

	Legislative	Executive	Judicial
Legislative		• can impeach a president • must give consent to going to war • can override a presidential veto • must approve international treaties	• can refuse to confirm a nominee to the Supreme Court • can impeach federal judges
Executive	• can veto any act of Congress • can call Congress into special session		• chooses whom to appoint to the Supreme Court
Judicial	• can declare a law unconstitutional	• can declare an executive order unconstitutional	

One other important aspect of the checks and balances is the **party system.** Throughout most of its history, the United States has been a nation of political parties. A political party is a group of people whose ideas about government are similar.

Today, there are two major political parties, Democrats and Republicans. Senators and representatives often refuse to support bills proposed by members of the opposing party. This means that debate, argument, and persuasion play a very important role in making the laws.

The party system also provides additional checks and balances between Congress and the president. If the president is a Democrat and Congress has Republican majorities in one or both houses, neither side can count on support from the other one. The president is more likely to veto bills, and Congress is more likely to refuse to confirm the president's judicial nominations. The two sides must work harder to do their jobs when they are of opposing political parties.

Name _____ Date _____

Federal Government Checkup

☆☆☆☆☆☆☆☆☆☆☆☆☆☆☆☆☆☆☆☆☆☆☆☆☆☆☆☆☆☆

Answer the questions.

1. What are the three branches of the federal government? _____

2. Why did the framers of the Constitution want a government with three branches?

   _____

   _____

3. What are the main responsibilities of Congress? _____

   _____

4. Which branch of the federal government is not elected by the voters?

   _____

5. What powers does the president have over Congress and the Supreme Court?

   _____

   _____

6. What are the two chambers of Congress called? _____

7. What power do ordinary citizens have in the government? _____

   _____

8. What powers does the Supreme Court have over Congress and the president?

   _____

   _____

9. How does a bill in Congress become a law? _____

   _____

   _____

10. How does the party system affect the way the government works?

    _____

    _____

    _____

Name _____   Date _____

Separation of Powers

☆☆☆☆☆☆☆☆☆☆☆☆☆☆☆☆☆☆☆☆☆☆☆☆☆☆☆☆☆☆☆☆☆☆☆

      The Federal Bureau of Investigation, or FBI, is part of the Department of Justice. The Department of Justice is part of the executive branch of the federal government. In the late 1940s, Congress wanted to use the FBI to investigate possible communist activities in the government. The cartoon suggests that President Truman would not allow such use. This cartoon was drawn by Clifford Berryman in 1948.

Study the cartoon and answer the questions.

Hope This Won't Develop into a Neighborhood Feud
Source: National Archives and Records Administration—Published May 18, 1948

1. When was this political cartoon first published? _____

2. Who do the two men in the cartoon represent? _____

3. What does the fence in the cartoon represent? _____

4. Why does President Truman tell Congress to stay on its side of the fence?

    _____

    _____

5. Why is the separation of powers in the federal government important?

    _____

    _____

State Government

To some extent, every state government is different. This is a tradition that dates back to the earliest days of the European settlement of North America. The thirteen original British colonies were all founded at different times and under different charters. Each colony had a distinct and different form of government. They were similar, but not identical.

The framers of the Constitution agreed that the federal government would have some powers and the states would have the rest. Each of the thirteen colonies already had a constitution. Every new territory that wants to become a state must present its constitution for approval to Congress before statehood is granted.

State governments take charge of details of public services that the federal government cannot easily deal with because it is too far away. A state government is local and is therefore directly in touch with the people who live in that state. State governments are responsible for such things as traffic laws, public school systems, and certain environmental regulations. State governments assess taxes on citizens to help pay for services. Each state is also responsible for running national and local elections.

The state government is similar to the federal government in structure. It has legislative, executive, and judicial branches. At the state level, the people vote directly for all government officials.

The chief executive of the state is the **governor.** Each state constitution specifies the qualifications of age, citizenship, and residency that a candidate for governor must meet. The second person in command is the **lieutenant governor,** who will take over for the governor in case of death or emergency.

The legislative branch is called the **state legislature.** Forty-nine of the fifty states have a bicameral legislature with a senate and a house of representatives. Each state has a different number of state senators and representatives.

★ PRESIDENTIAL ★ TRIVIA

MARTIN VAN BUREN (1782–1862)

Martin Van Buren was the eighth president of the United States. He served from 1837 to 1841. He was the first U.S. president born in a state. The seven presidents before him were born when America was a colony of Great Britain.

The Federal System (The Division of Powers)

Federal Government	Both Federal and State Governments	State Governments
1. Has enumerated powers	1. Have concurrent powers	1. Have reserved powers
2. President leads executive branch	2. Have constitutions	2. Governor leads executive branch
3. U.S. Congress makes laws	3. Have three branches	3. Legislative body makes laws
4. U.S. Supreme Court is highest court	4. Can collect taxes	4. Have state courts
5. Can send army into war	5. Have court systems	5. Make public school laws
6. Prints money	6. Provide services	6. Set marriage and driving age
7. Capital at Washington, D.C.		

Research State Government

☆☆☆☆☆☆☆☆☆☆☆☆☆☆☆☆☆☆☆☆☆☆☆☆☆☆☆☆☆☆☆☆

Complete the following activity.

Use the Internet to find your state's home page. Use the information you find online to answer the following questions about your state. If you wish, you can research a state of your choice instead of your home state.

1. My state is _____.

2. The governor of my state is _____.

3. My state became a state in the year _____.

4. My state's constitution was written in the year _____.

5. The state constitution was last amended in the year _____.

6. How many senators and representatives are in the state legislature? _____

7. How do those numbers relate to the total population of the state?

   _____

   _____

8. What are the qualifications for serving as governor?

   _____

   _____

9. What are the qualifications for serving in the state legislature?

   _____

   _____

10. What is one important service that your state government provides to the people?

    _____

    _____

    _____

    _____

11. The nation was founded by men who strongly disagreed over which should have more power: the national government or the state governments. In the end, they tried to achieve a compromise. How successful do you think they were? On a separate sheet of paper, write a short essay giving your opinion.

Local Government

There are almost as many types of local government in the United States as there are communities. Big cities have highly structured governments that mirror the organization of the state government. Small towns and sparsely settled rural areas have very few government officials.

Local governments are responsible for making and enforcing laws and providing services, just as state and national governments are. The difference is that a local government is tailored very specifically to meet the needs of a much smaller number of people. A group of people who live in the same small geographical area have many concerns in common that people outside that area do not share. This is the reason for local government.

PRESIDENTIAL TRIVIA

Since 1788, more and more Americans have lived in cities. However, almost all U.S. presidents have come from small towns and rural areas. Only Theodore Roosevelt, William Taft, John Kennedy, and Gerald Ford were born in large cities.

Government in the Big City

Millions of people live in the nation's largest cities, such as New York, Chicago, and Los Angeles. The governments of these big cities are headed by an executive called the **mayor.** The legislative branch the mayor must work with is called the **council.** In most cities, the voters directly elect both the mayor and the city council members. A city is normally divided into several districts, with one city council member per district. Districts are based on the size of the population, so that the council represents everyone equally. The responsibilities of and the relationship between the mayor and the city council are very much like those of the president and Congress.

Government in the Town

Many small towns have no official governments of their own. They do not need such highly structured governments, because they are smaller than big cities. Instead, voters attend annual meetings at which they elect board members, pass laws, and set tax rates. The members of the town board serve as the town government during the rest of the year, between meetings. This form of government has existed since the early days of New England and still exists today in small communities.

Government in the County

Almost every state is divided geographically into **counties.** Each county has its own government, headed by a **county board.** These county officials are directly elected by the people.

Name _____ Date _____

Your Local Government

☆☆☆☆☆☆☆☆☆☆☆☆☆☆☆☆☆☆☆☆☆☆☆☆☆☆☆☆☆☆☆☆☆

Complete the following activity.

Create a presentation that illustrates the structure of your local government. You may work with a partner or with a group. Follow these steps:

1. Identify the type of community you live in. Is it a major city like Boston or Dallas? Is it a small city or a town? Is it a rural area?

2. Find out who your local government officials are. You can study the government section in your telephone book or search for the information online.

3. Answer the following questions:

   • What is the structure of the local government?

   • What are the important responsibilities of the officials?

   • How long are their terms of office?

4. Once you have acquired a good working knowledge of your local government, it's time to put together your presentation. The object is to help the class understand how your community is governed.

5. Use computer software, poster board, or other resources to organize your material and create visual elements such as organizational charts and outlines.

6. Present your talk to the class. Afterward, hold a question-and-answer session on your local government and how it works.

7. If possible, ask a local government official to visit the class.

Two Plans of Mayor-City Council Government

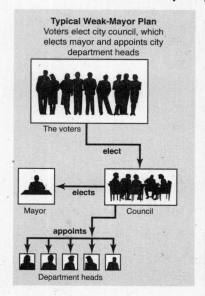

Typical Weak-Mayor Plan
Voters elect city council, which elects mayor and appoints city department heads

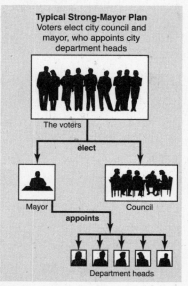

Typical Strong-Mayor Plan
Voters elect city council and mayor, who appoints city department heads

Leaders

Imagine if everyone voted on every decision made by a government or organization. People would be voting all the time! Instead, people choose leaders to make decisions and take care of the business of government. In politics, the leaders might be individuals like the president. Or, the leaders might be representatives elected to make the laws and run the government.

What makes a good leader? Most people agree on some important qualities. A good leader creates a vision or idea that other people can believe in. He or she can communicate that vision so that people want to achieve it together. A leader is a person who is able to bring about major changes in society. A leader does this by caring about change and working to make it happen.

An effective leader acts honestly. She or he can accept criticism and admit a mistake. A great leader can adjust to new situations. He or she can handle bad news and keep cool under pressure. Great leaders make tough and sensible decisions.

Successful leaders are **competent.** That means they have the skills necessary to do the job. However, they also need a sense of right and wrong in order to use those skills properly.

Not all leaders are politicians. Some leaders influence governments without ever winning an election. Mahatma Gandhi led a successful nonviolent movement to free India from British rule. Martin Luther King, Jr., fought for civil rights in the United States. Elizabeth Cady Stanton succeeded in expanding women's rights in the United States in the 1800s.

Leadership comes in many forms. Sometimes leaders can be great military figures. Joan of Arc inspired the people of France in the Middle Ages. Sitting Bull fought with dignity to preserve Native American rights in the late 1800s.

You can also find leaders among working men and women. During the industry boom of the nineteenth and early twentieth centuries, most factory workers were paid very low wages. Working conditions were unsafe. Hours were long. Many courageous workers fought for their rights. They created labor unions that officially represented the workers in their struggle for fair hours and wages. César Chávez is a good example of a worker who rose from the ranks to become a leader. A migrant worker himself, Chávez led the struggle for fair wages and reasonable protections for all migrant workers in the Southwest. Leaders who fight for change risk losing their jobs and even their lives because they are standing up to people with power. Leaders must place their goals for the future before their personal safety and security.

★ PRESIDENTIAL ★
TRIVIA

Important U.S. leaders do not always become president. Henry Clay, Daniel Webster, and John Calhoun led U.S. politics between 1810 and 1850. They were all excellent speakers. All three desperately wanted to become president. None was ever elected. Henry Clay lost three separate times: 1824, 1832, and 1840.

Name _____ Date _____

Describe a Leader

☆☆☆☆☆☆☆☆☆☆☆☆☆☆☆☆☆☆☆☆☆☆☆☆☆☆☆☆☆☆☆☆☆☆

Complete the following activity.

What are the qualities that make a good leader? Why are these qualities important to someone governing a nation?

Choose a political leader whom you admire from one of the following categories:

- a government official such as Representative Barbara Jordan

- a religious leader such as Martin Luther King, Jr.

- a political activist such as Emma Goldman

- an international statesman such as Kofi Annan

- a labor leader such as Lech Walesa

You may choose a person from past history or someone who is prominent in today's political world.

Use the library and/or the Internet to research this leader's life and career.

Write an essay explaining why you admire this person, what his or her major achievements were, and why you believe he or she was/is a great leader. Take notes for your essay below.

1. Name of person: _____

2. Positions held: _____

_____

3. Major achievements: _____

_____

_____

_____

_____

4. Reasons this person was/is a great leader: _____

_____

_____

_____

_____

President

The president of the United States is one of the most powerful leaders in the world. The president's oath of office reads as follows:

> I, [president's name], do solemnly swear that I will faithfully execute the office of President of the United States; and will, to the best of my ability, preserve, protect, and defend the Constitution of the United States, so help me God.

The president is the head of state. He or she must confer with the rulers of other nations and work out all international agreements. The president appoints ambassadors to foreign countries. The president nominates judges to the Supreme Court.

The president also takes part in the process of making laws. Once Congress has approved a bill, the president must sign it in order for it to become law. The president can **veto** any bill he opposes. It takes a two-thirds majority of Congress to overturn a presidential veto.

The Constitution states that the president must be a U.S. citizen from birth and must have lived in the U.S. for at least 14 years. He or she must be at least 35 years old. The youngest presidents in history were Theodore Roosevelt, who was only 42 when he took office, and John F. Kennedy, who was 43 when he was elected in November 1960. The oldest president was Ronald Reagan, who was 69 when he took office in 1981. He served two terms.

The president serves a four-year term. He must then run for reelection. Originally, there was no limit to the number of terms a president could serve. This changed in 1951 when Congress passed the Twenty-second Amendment, limiting presidents to two terms in office.

Through the 2004 elections, all presidents of the United States have been men. However, the Constitution uses the word *person* to describe the president. Any woman who meets the qualifications of age, residency, and citizenship can run for president.

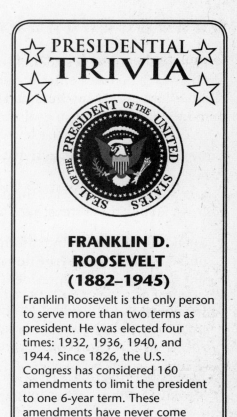

PRESIDENTIAL TRIVIA

FRANKLIN D. ROOSEVELT (1882–1945)

Franklin Roosevelt is the only person to serve more than two terms as president. He was elected four times: 1932, 1936, 1940, and 1944. Since 1826, the U.S. Congress has considered 160 amendments to limit the president to one 6-year term. These amendments have never come close to passing.

Name _____ Date _____

Write and Deliver an Inaugural Address

  Although the president is elected in November, he does not take office until January 20. The day on which he takes office is called Inauguration Day. On that day, the new president takes the oath of office and delivers an **inaugural address** to the nation. This speech outlines the president's immediate and long-term goals for his first term in office.

Complete the following activity.

  Suppose that you are the new president of the United States. Write and deliver your inaugural address. Follow these steps:

1. Spend some time on the Internet and in the library identifying the most important national issues of the moment, and write down your position on each issue. Think about what changes you would like to bring about as president.

2. Go online or to the library to find inaugural addresses of past presidents. (HINT: The government publishes the complete presidential inaugural addresses every four years.) Skim through these speeches to see what past presidents have spoken about on their first day in office.

3. Remember that this is NOT a campaign speech; you are already president. The purposes of an inaugural address are as follows:

   • to honor the solemn occasion of a transfer of power in government

   • to rally the enthusiasm of the people

   • to describe your goals and intentions for your first term

   • to give the people an idea of who you are and how you will handle the job of being president

4. Draft your speech. Set an outside limit of two single-spaced typed pages. (George Washington's second inaugural address was only two paragraphs long!)

5. Review your draft. Make sure that it clearly says everything you want to say and that your ideas are organized in a logical and cogent order.

6. Write your final draft and deliver your speech to the class.

Vice President

The vice president's most important responsibility is to take over the office of the president if necessary. Several presidents have been assassinated or have died of natural causes while in office. In each case, the vice president has taken his place. A candidate for vice president must meet all the same qualifications as a presidential candidate.

The voters do not choose vice presidents. Instead, close advisers to a serious presidential candidate suggest good vice presidential choices, and the candidate makes this decision alone. The presidential candidate must find someone who will support the president's policies, be loyal to the president's decisions, and lead the nation as president if necessary. The vice president also serves as president of the Senate and can cast a tie-breaking vote.

The Twelfth Amendment (1804) declares that a president and vice president cannot be from the same home state. It has been common in modern times for the presidential candidate to choose someone from an entirely different region of the country than his own in order to appeal to more voters. For example, Richard Nixon of California chose Spiro Agnew of Maryland, and John F. Kennedy of Massachusetts chose Lyndon B. Johnson of Texas.

In many elections, there is more than one candidate for president from the same party. These candidates run against one another in primary elections. When one candidate emerges as the clear favorite of the voters in the party, he often asks one of the other strong candidates to be his vice president. This happened in 1992 when Bill Clinton chose Al Gore.

Once the president announces the choice of vice president, the two candidates then campaign together as **running mates.** Together, they are called the **ticket** of their political party. When citizens vote on Election Day, they must vote for the ticket. It is not possible to vote for a president from one ticket and a vice president from another.

Almost all presidents run for reelection. Many vice presidents run for president once the president leaves office.

PRESIDENTIAL TRIVIA

JOHN TYLER (1790–1862)

John Tyler was the first vice president to become president. He took the office in 1841 when President William Henry Harrison died just a few weeks after taking office.

Name _____   Date _____

Appoint a Vice President

☆☆☆☆☆☆☆☆☆☆☆☆☆☆☆☆☆☆☆☆☆☆☆☆☆☆☆☆☆☆☆☆☆

Complete the following activity.

When a vice president leaves office before the term is up, the president may appoint a new vice president, subject to confirmation by a majority of both houses of Congress. Suppose that the current vice president has resigned. Together, you and your classmates will role-play the process of choosing the new vice president. Follow these steps:

1. Work in a group of four people. Together, decide on a list of five or six likely candidates. You should look at cabinet members, members of Congress, governors, and prominent political figures not currently in office. These are all likely places for a president to look when choosing his successor.

2. Each group member should take one or two of the candidates and write up a brief resume/description of where the person stands on the important issues. You can find out much of this information at www.house.gov, www.senate.gov, and in the online archives of major newspapers such as the *New York Times* and the *Wall Street Journal*.

3. Make copies of the information and give them to every person in the group. Overnight, read the information and think about who would be the best choice for vice president.

4. Meet the next day. As the president's closest advisers, discuss which candidate is the best choice. Each member of the group should defend his or her choice based on facts and evidence. The four of you need not come to a consensus; you must be clear on which candidate you support and why.

5. Finally, choose which of you will play the role of the president. The president must choose among the candidates suggested by the advisers. The president must then present his or her choice to Congress (the rest of the class) for approval. He or she must defend his or her decision with a strong, well-supported argument. (This speech should take no more than five minutes.)

6. The rest of the students, representing Congress, then meet as a committee-of-the-whole to debate and vote on the president's nomination. A simple majority is required for the nominee to be confirmed.

Senator

The **Senate** is the upper house of the United States Congress. As you have read, Congress is the legislative branch of the federal government.

The writers of the Constitution created the U.S. Senate to give power to people from less-populated states. In the Senate, each state is represented equally. The people of each of the 50 states elect 2 senators. The U.S. Senate has 100 senators. It does not matter if the states are large or small. In 2000, California's population was more than 33 million, while Wyoming's was less than 1 million. Yet both states had 2 senators.

The vice president serves as president of the Senate. If a Senate vote is tied, the vice president can break the tie with his vote.

A senator serves a 6-year term. Every 2 years, about one-third of the senators' terms expire. This ensures that at least two-thirds of the members of the Senate will at all times be experienced. It is important to have continuity in the Senate because it has so much power in the government. Senators can serve as many terms as their constituents want. Unlike the Senate, the entire House of Representatives is up for election every 2 years. This also means that the Senate is not as affected by immediate public opinion as the House of Representatives is.

A senator must be at least 30 years old and must have been a U.S. citizen for at least 9 years. A senator must also live in the state from which he or she is elected. However, each state makes its own rules about how long a senator must have lived there.

Until 1913, senators were chosen by the state legislatures. The people had no say in who would represent them in the Senate. This changed during the Progressive Era, a time of political reform that officially began in 1912 with the creation of the Progressive Party. The Progressives wanted to eliminate corruption in politics and give the people more say. They fought for the passage of the Seventeenth Amendment, which declares that senators are to be elected directly by the people. This amendment became law in 1913. The effect was that U.S. government became more democratic.

PRESIDENTIAL TRIVIA

LYNDON B. JOHNSON (1908–1973)

President Lyndon B. Johnson came to the presidency with several years' experience as Senate Majority Leader. As president, he used his impressive negotiating skills to persuade Congress to pass a group of important social programs known as the "Great Society." Many senators and representatives had doubts about such programs as Head Start and Medicare, but Johnson always knew how to find the votes he needed to get his programs passed.

Debate the Status of Washingtonians

The nation's capital, Washington, D.C., is not within one of the fifty states. It occupies a piece of land on the Maryland-Virginia border. Since Washington, D.C., is not a state, its citizens do not share some of the ordinary rights and privileges of all other Americans.

Washington, D.C., has no senator and only one representative in Congress. The representative is not a voting member. He or she may participate in debate but cannot vote on bills, confirmations of presidential appointments, or on any other matter before the Senate or the House.

Complete the following activity.

With a partner, debate the fairness of the political status of the residents of Washington, D.C. Consider these factors:

- What is the population of Washington, D.C.?

- What does it mean for the citizens of Washington, D.C., that they are not represented in the Senate and that their representative in Congress lacks voting privileges?

- Would it be fair for Washingtonians to have the same rights as all other citizens even though they do not live in one of the fifty states?

- The territories of Guam and American Samoa and the commonwealth of Puerto Rico also have non-voting Congressional representatives. Puerto Ricans are U.S. citizens. Is it right that Washingtonians do not have greater rights and privileges than Puerto Ricans?

You and your partner should each take one side of the question. One should argue that the current situation is perfectly right and reasonable. The other should argue for change.

Both of you must use facts and evidence to defend your positions. The partner arguing for change should have some ideas about what changes should be made and how they would be implemented.

Representative

The **House of Representatives,** usually just called "the House," is the lower house of Congress. Congress has two houses so that both the states and the people can be represented fairly.

When the Constitution was written, delegates from the smaller states were worried that larger states would have too much power. Those from the larger states argued that it was fair for their states to have more power because they represented more people. The framers of the Constitution resolved the argument by creating both a House and a Senate. In the Senate, each state is represented equally, so large states cannot overpower small ones. In the House, the states are represented according to their **population,** so small states cannot overpower large ones.

The population of the United States is officially counted once every 10 years in a **census.** The government uses the census results to determine how many representatives each state will get in the House. The House currently has 435 voting members. Larger states have more representatives than smaller states do. Each state is guaranteed at least one representative.

This chart shows a sampling of states, their population as of the 2001 census, and their number of representatives.

PRESIDENTIAL TRIVIA

JOHN QUINCY ADAMS (1767–1848)

Several representatives have been elected president, but only one man ever did the opposite. When President John Quincy Adams lost his bid for reelection, he ran for Congress. Adams represented Massachusetts in the House for over 17 years, arguing forcefully for the abolition of slavery. Adams died on the floor of the House in 1848.

State	Population	Number of Representatives
Kansas	2,688,418	4
Connecticut	3,405,565	5
Michigan	9,938,444	15
Pennsylvania	12,281,054	19
New York	18,976,457	29
California	33,871,648	53

Source: *New York Times Almanac 2006,* p. 269: data from U.S. Bureau of the Census, 2001.

Representatives serve two-year terms. Every representative's term expires at the same time. It is possible in theory to have an entirely new House once every two years. In fact, representatives are often reelected. Their constituents have come to know them and often feel that they have done a good job.

A candidate for the House must be at least 25 years old and must have been a U.S. citizen for at least 7 years. Representatives have always been elected by direct popular vote.

Name _____ Date _____

Read a Political Map

☆☆☆☆☆☆☆☆☆☆☆☆☆☆☆☆☆☆☆☆☆☆☆☆☆☆☆☆☆☆☆☆

This map shows how many members each state sends to the House of Representatives.

Apportionment of the U.S. House of Representatives for the 108th Congress Based on the 2000 Census

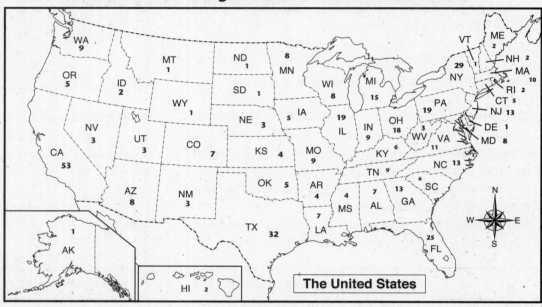

Use the map to answer the questions.

1. Which is the largest state in the United States by population? How do you know?

_____

2. Which is the smallest? How do you know?

_____

_____

3. You know that each state has 2 senators. If you add 2 to the number of representatives shown for each state, you get that state's number of **electoral votes.** These are the votes assigned to candidates in presidential elections. A candidate must get a minimum of 270 electoral votes to win the election. Use the map to determine the least number of states a candidate can win to get 270 electoral votes. List the states and the number of votes per state.

_____

_____

_____

_____

Representative
Cast Your Vote HS, SV 9781419036378

Name _____   Date _____

Write to Your Representative

☆☆☆☆☆☆☆☆☆☆☆☆☆☆☆☆☆☆☆☆☆☆☆☆☆☆☆☆☆☆☆☆☆☆☆☆

Complete the following activity.

Use the Internet, your school library, and other resources to find the following information. You may work alone or with a partner. (HINT: An excellent Internet resource is www.house.gov.)

1. My home state is _____.

2. My state has _____ representatives in Congress.

3. The name and number of my congressional district is _____.

4. My representative in Congress is _____.

Find a current issue that concerns you. Talk to your parents or other adults you know well, watch the news, and read newspapers and news magazines to find an issue.

5. Issue that concerns me: _____

6. Why this issue concerns me: _____
   _____
   _____

7. Tell how to contact your representative:

   a. by e-mail: _____

   b. by regular mail: _____

8. Write a letter to your representative about the issue you have chosen. Explain why this issue interests you and urge your representative to support your side.

9. Go over your letter with your teacher, a parent, or another adult you know well. Make sure that it follows the proper format for a business letter.

10. Mail your letter. If you receive a response, share it with the class.

Name _____   Date _____

Power to the People

☆☆☆☆☆☆☆☆☆☆☆☆☆☆☆☆☆☆☆☆☆☆☆☆☆☆☆☆☆☆☆☆☆☆☆

     To try to make Congress more modern and effective, the Legislative Reorganization Act of 1946 was passed. At the time, Sam Rayburn was the Speaker of the House, and Alben Barkley was the Majority Leader of the Senate. The act did several things. It reduced the number of congressional committees and authorized professional staff members. In the end, the act did reorganize Congress, but it did not make the legislative body much more effective or responsive to the public. The cartoon below is about the Legislative Reorganization Act of 1946. It was drawn by Clifford Berryman.

Study the cartoon and answer the questions.

Source: National Archives and Records Administration—Published July 28, 1946

1. When was this political cartoon first published? _____

2. The two seated men are Barkley and Rayburn. Who is the standing man? _____

   Whom does he represent? _____

3. What kind of reorganization is John Q. Public talking about? _____

4. Why does John Q. Public say his reorganization will take place in November?

   _____

5. In the United States, the people are supposed to have power over their government. Do you believe that this is true? Why or why not?

   _____

   _____

Cast Your Vote HS, SV 9781419036378

Governor and State Legislators

The United States is a **federal** republic. The word *federal* means that authority is shared between the national government and the state governments. There is no direct chain of command between the governor of a state and the president of the United States.

Each state has its own constitution, and each state is self-governing. However, each state must abide by the laws of the U.S. Constitution. If it does not, the national government can step in to force compliance. This happened during the civil rights movement of the 1960s. The national government took charge of state-run elections in Southern states to ensure that African Americans would not be intimidated or driven away from polling places.

The **governor** is the chief executive of the state. Governors of most states are required to be at least 25 to 30 years old and to be residents of the state in which they are running for election. They are directly elected by the people and generally serve four-year terms. In some states, such as New York, governors are limited to two terms. In other states, such as Arkansas, they can stay in office as long as the citizens continue to vote for them.

The governor is in charge of carrying out the state's laws. He or she must choose people to be in charge of state departments and agencies. Governors usually work with state legislatures to suggest new laws. Governors help to plan the state's budget. In some states, they have the power to veto laws passed by the legislature.

The governor is also the public face of the state. He or she must meet regularly with the media and present issues that are important to the state. The governor appears at important occasions and ceremonies.

The governor is also the head, or "commander-in-chief," of the state's **National Guard.** The National Guard is the military reserves recruited by the states and equipped by the federal government. In the case of a state emergency—such as a blizzard, flood, or riot—the governor can call on the National Guard for help.

The **lieutenant governor** is the second-highest executive officer in a state. The lieutenant governor is to the governor as the vice president is to the president. The lieutenant governor replaces the governor if he or she dies or resigns. In some states, the lieutenant governor is the leader of a part of the legislature. Some states do not even have a lieutenant governor.

The seat of state government is located in the state capital. The state capital is not always the largest city in the state.

PRESIDENTIAL TRIVIA

FRANKLIN D. ROOSEVELT (1882–1945)

Franklin D. Roosevelt was governor of New York from 1928 until his election to the presidency in 1932. Roosevelt was an enormously effective governor despite his physical disability. A severe attack of polio had left him unable to walk more than a few steps, and then only on crutches. Roosevelt's strong, confident personality belied his handicap. He remains the only person ever elected to four terms as president.

Governor and State Legislators, continued

Each state has a legislature in which all **counties** are equally represented. All states except Nebraska have a bicameral legislature like the U.S. Congress, with a senate and a house of representatives. (Nebraska's legislature has been **unicameral** since 1937.) Age requirements vary by state, but most states require legislators to be U.S. citizens age 21 or older who live in the districts they represent. Most state senators serve four-year terms, and most representatives two-year terms.

Everyone in the state can vote for governor, but people can vote only for legislators from their own district. If a governor represents one political party and the majority of the legislators represent the other party, state government becomes a challenge.

In some states, state legislators may work only part-time. In other states, the work can be more time-consuming. The main job of state legislators is to make the state a better place to live. They do this by passing new laws and considering ideas suggested by other state legislators.

The state legislature is usually in charge of writing or approving the state's budget. The legislature also decides the state tax rate. This tax money supports public institutions like state colleges and the workings of state government.

Citizens can play a greater direct role in their state government than they can in the national government. Here are three ways for citizens to take part in making state laws:

- **Initiative.** Citizens can propose laws and then gather signatures on a petition. If they collect enough signatures, the proposed law will appear on the ballot, and the people can vote directly to pass or defeat it.

- **Referendum.** Certain laws passed by the state legislature are placed on the ballot for overturning or approval by direct popular vote.

- **Recall.** Many states have recall provisions, in which citizens can propose that an unpopular government official be removed from office. If protestors gather enough support, a recall election is held. Other candidates are free to run against the incumbent. If the incumbent is defeated in a recall election, he or she must leave office.

PRESIDENTIAL TRIVIA

ABRAHAM LINCOLN (1809–1865)

Most people consider Abraham Lincoln to be one of the greatest presidents in U.S. history. However, Lincoln did not have much official experience. He served only four terms in the Illinois state legislature and a single term in the U.S. House of Representatives.

Debate States' Rights

You have read that the United States is a federal republic. The Constitution states that all powers not directly granted to the federal government remain with the states or the people.

By the time the original 13 British colonies became the United States, they were accustomed to having independent governments. No state was eager to cede any of its power to another state. Therefore, the framers of the Constitution left a great deal of power with the individual states.

Throughout U.S. history, a fierce debate has continued between those who believe the national government should have greater control over the states and those who believe the national government should never interfere with a state's right to govern itself.

Complete the following activity.

Your job is to debate the issue of states' rights versus the rights of the national government. Follow these steps:

1. Form two teams of six. One team will argue in favor of states' rights. The other will argue for a stronger role for the national government.

2. Read the U.S. Constitution to see what it says about states' rights.

3. Go online or to the library to find out about times in U.S. history that states' rights have clashed with national laws. These include:

   • the period leading up to the Civil War of 1861–1865

   • the Progressive Era in the early 1900s

   • the civil rights movement of the 1960s

4. Find your state's home page on the Internet and read about state government and the types of issues it deals with. Compare this to the issues dealt with by the White House and Congress.

5. Have a discussion with your team members. Work together to articulate your reasons for supporting or opposing states' rights. Use facts and evidence from your research.

6. Stage your debate in front of the class. You are free to refer to written notes as needed. After the debate, include the rest of the class in a discussion with questions and answers.

Mayor and Council

The most important local government officials in the United States are the **mayors** of large cities. They represent millions of people and work with much larger economies and budgets than some entire states. For example, New York City alone has a larger population (eight million) than 40 of the 50 states.

The mayor is elected directly by the voters of the city, not by the entire state. For example, the only Pennsylvanians who vote for the mayors of Philadelphia and Pittsburgh are residents of those cities. Many people who work in major cities but live outside the city limits are affected daily by the mayor's decisions and policies. However, they cannot vote for him or her.

Mayors are generally elected to four-year terms. In some cities, mayors are limited to two terms in office. Philadelphia and New York are two examples of cities with mayoral term limits.

Large cities are divided into districts. Each district has its own **city council** member. Large cities may also have several at-large members who do not represent specific districts. The city council is to the mayor as Congress is to the president of the United States.

City council members are concerned strictly with local issues. Each city council member will support legislation that is best for his or her own district and the city as a whole. Suppose that the city is proposing to shut down a farmers' market to build a new mass-transit station, or to undertake a large construction project in your neighborhood. If you strongly support or oppose such a project, you can appeal to your city council member for help.

A city council member maintains an office in his or her district. It is generally very easy to make direct contact with your city council representative. The mayor has his or her office in the **city hall.**

PRESIDENTIAL TRIVIA

Many presidents have served in the legislature or as governor. However, only three have been mayors. Andrew Johnson was mayor of Greeneville, Tennessee (1834–1838), Grover Cleveland was mayor of Buffalo, New York (1881–1883), and Calvin Coolidge was mayor of Northampton, Massachusetts (1910–1911). Of the three, only Buffalo is a large city.

Name _____ Date _____

Write an Editorial

    An **editorial** is a special type of persuasive essay. It states the writer's position on a social or political issue and backs it up with facts and evidence. The editorial writer's job is to persuade readers to agree with his or her position. All major newspapers have a daily page called the Op-Ed page, short for Opinion-Editorial.

    Politicians and government officials read newspapers, too. They know that a newspaper's editorial support is important to a candidate running for election or reelection.

Complete the following activity.

    Write an editorial praising or criticizing a recent action of the mayor, the city council, or the two together. Follow these steps:

1. Read the local papers, search the Internet, and listen to news on the radio and television for a few days. Learn about the recent decisions and activities of the mayor and the city council. Choose an issue or action about which you feel strongly. Here are examples of the kinds of issues you may find:

   - a proposed citywide ban on smoking in public places

   - city involvement in planning and funding a major real estate development along the waterfront

   - support for a citywide curbside recycling program

   - choice of a location for a new baseball stadium

2. Gather enough facts about the issue to back up your opinion on it. Consider the economic effect on the city, the impact the issue has on the daily lives of the people, and the greater impact the issue may have on the entire state. Read the newspapers and search for information online. Talk to your classmates and to adults you know well to find out what other people think and why they feel as they do about this issue.

3. Write a sentence that clearly states your position on the issue.

4. Draft your editorial. Include facts and evidence that will persuade your readers to agree with your position. Avoid using loaded words and emotional language. Maintain a neutral tone and stick to the facts. This will make your editorial much more persuasive.

5. After your teacher has read and commented on your editorial, write a final version. Submit it for publication in the school newspaper. You may also want to submit it to local newspapers, so that adults of voting age will read it and be influenced.

Political Parties

People elected to office usually belong to a **political party.** A political party is a group of people organized to support certain beliefs about national policy. Members of political parties work together to reach their goals. They try to help candidates from their party to win elections.

There are two major political parties in the United States. They are the Republican Party and the Democratic Party. Both parties want to help and protect the country. They both work on the national, state, and local levels. The Democrats and Republicans have alternated in power since the Civil War. However, there were other major political parties before 1860 such as the Whigs and the Federalists.

The United States is sometimes said to have a two-party system. However, nothing in the Constitution requires two parties. In fact, there is nothing in the Constitution about political parties at all. Minor parties, sometimes called **"third parties,"** have often played an important role in U.S. politics. Third parties direct voters' attention to issues that the major parties want to avoid. Sometimes, a third party gains its goals by supporting a major party. The major party then acts on the third party's views.

In most states, a person can join a political party when registering to vote. Political parties have both paid and unpaid workers. However, a person does not have to join a political party. A person who does not belong to a political party is sometimes called an **independent.**

People in a democracy often disagree about what the government should do. Political parties provide a way for voters to easily identify a candidate's positions.

PRESIDENTIAL TRIVIA

GEORGE WASHINGTON (1732–1799)

George Washington is the only president in U.S. history who refused to get involved in party politics. When Washington was elected, there were no political parties in the U.S. Although they quickly began to develop, Washington disapproved of them and did not represent any party. He remains the only president who was the universal choice of all the political leaders of his day.

Name _____   Date _____

Research U.S. Political Parties

      Today, the two major parties in U.S. politics are the Democratic and Republican parties. However, this was not always true. Neither of these two parties existed when the country was founded. Other major political parties have disappeared or changed their names over time. There have also been important, though short-lived, third parties.

Complete the following activity.

      Choose a U.S. political party and write a short paper describing its history. Follow these steps:

1. Find a current issue of the *New York Times Almanac,* which is published every year. Look at the section on U.S. presidents. The *Almanac* lists presidents by their political party. It also gives breakdowns of the vote for every presidential election, including a listing of all major candidates and their political parties.

2. Choose a political party to research. In addition to the Democrats and Republicans, choices include the Whigs, the Federalists, the Bull Moose Party, the Progressives, and several others. Go online and/or to the library to find out more about the party and its history.

3. Take notes on the articles you read. Ask questions such as the following:
   - When and how did the party come into being?
   - Who were the party's founders and major candidates?
   - Which major issues of the day made people create this political party?
   - Did this party ever win a presidential election?
   - Is the party still in existence? If not, when and why did it disappear?
   - Why is the party important to understanding U.S. history?

4. Write your paper. It should be two to three full pages. You may want to add a time line or other graphics that will help your reader understand your party's history.

5. Form a small group with other students who have researched the same political party. Some of you may have found out different facts or come to different conclusions. Discuss your facts and ideas.

6. Share the results of your research and discussion with the class.

Candidates

To run for president, a person must make a formal announcement. This is called "throwing one's hat into the ring." The candidate must gather a staff of supporters and volunteers who will run the national campaign.

Some people who run for president choose to do so from the first. Others are "drafted" by supporters who believe their candidate is the only one who can rescue the nation from its current problems. These supporters may be the candidate's political party, or his or her prominent and powerful friends and associates.

The Constitution states three simple qualifications for the office of president. A person must be a natural-born U.S. citizen who is at least 35 years old and who has lived in the U.S. for at least 14 years. Millions of people meet these qualifications, but very few have a real chance of being elected president. Any successful candidate must also have the ability to raise millions of dollars for a campaign.

To find out if they are likely to be able to raise sufficient funds, candidates often form **exploratory committees** as early as two years before the presidential election. Committee members look for support from corporations, labor unions, professional associations, and wealthy individuals. If the situation looks promising, the committee will advise the candidate to go ahead. Occasionally an immensely wealthy person, such as Steve Forbes or Ross Perot, runs for president. These candidates pay for their campaigns from their personal fortunes.

Typical presidential candidates include governors, senators, representatives, mayors of large cities, and prominent military leaders. These people have experience in leadership roles. They have important contacts within their political party and with powerful people across the nation.

Presidential candidates who are already famous in public life have a tremendous advantage in a campaign. Voters are more likely to listen to and support someone they feel they "know," even if only from a distance. This is the reason **incumbent** candidates are often reelected. The voters are familiar with them and know how they perform on the job. Voters often prefer a known quantity to an unknown candidate who may or may not meet their expectations.

PRESIDENTIAL TRIVIA

A famous myth is that anyone can be president. However, most U.S. presidents were not poor. Actually, about half the presidents have come from very wealthy families. Some, including John Kennedy and George Washington, ranked among the richest people in the country.

Choosing a Candidate

☆☆☆☆☆☆☆☆☆☆☆☆☆☆☆☆☆☆☆☆☆☆☆☆☆☆☆☆☆☆☆☆☆☆☆☆

A variety of people run for president. Some throw their hat into the ring as early as two years before a presidential election. Others are talked about on the news as possible candidates even before they make any announcement. This talk can persist despite a person's refusal to make a commitment to running.

Complete the following activity.

Decide which of the current candidates is the best person for the job. Follow these steps:

1. Find out who is most likely to run for president in the upcoming election. This includes people who have announced that they will run and people who seem very likely to make such an announcement. This information is readily available on television, on the Internet, and in major newspapers. Make a list of the candidates.

_____

_____

_____

_____

_____

2. Do research on each candidate. Find out about his or her background, experience, and public record. If any of the candidates are currently serving in Congress, each will have his or her own page at www.house.gov or www.senate.gov. If they have formally thrown their hat into the ring, they will almost certainly have set up Web pages for their campaigns.

3. Write a short essay explaining who you think is the best candidate for president. Explain what qualities are important to you in choosing a candidate to support and how this particular candidate embodies those qualities.

4. Share your essay with the class.

Campaigning

A presidential campaign can begin up to two years before the general election. Just after the November 2006 elections, candidates for the 2008 presidential election began to declare their intention to run for president.

During the many months that lead up to the general election, candidates try to get their message to as many voters as possible. This means they must travel across the country, especially once the series of primary elections begins (several months before the summer nominating conventions). Candidates usually spend more time in larger states because more electoral votes are at stake there. However, they make a genuine effort to cover the entire country.

A presidential campaign includes many important aspects.

Staff and Volunteers

A nationwide campaign requires a large staff and thousands of volunteers. Candidates have headquarters in every state. Volunteers staff these headquarters. Some of their duties include:

- making telephone calls to registered voters
- answering questions about the candidate's schedule
- preparing and sending out mailings
- organizing local appearances by the candidate
- organizing rallies and fundraisers for the candidate
- helping to register voters

Volunteers receive no pay for their efforts. However, they gain valuable experience and an inside look at the political system. Many prominent politicians began their careers as student volunteers.

Advertising

Many things come under the general heading of advertising. These include buttons, direct mailings, telephone appeals, television and radio commercials, and Web pages.

Campaign advertisements fall into two categories:

1. Ads that praise the candidate mention high points in his or her public record and suggest that he or she is the best person for the job.

2. **Attack ads** slant information to make the opponent look as bad as possible. They take statements out of context to use against the opponent. This approach is known as **negative campaigning.** Major newspapers analyze attack ads and point out inaccuracies. Most voters claim to dislike negative campaigning. However, attack ads continue to be used in many campaigns. Some attack ads even attack candidates for negative campaigning.

PRESIDENTIAL TRIVIA

Senator John F. Kennedy and Vice President Richard Nixon made history during the 1960 presidential campaign by participating in the first presidential debates that were broadcast live on both radio and TV. Many voters were impressed with Kennedy's grasp of important national issues and with his relaxed, confident manner. Nixon, by contrast, seemed defensive, nervous, and uncomfortable. Historians believe that these debates were an important turning point in Kennedy's favor. He would go on to win the presidential election by a narrow margin.

Campaigning, continued

Personal Appearances and Interviews

Candidates try to meet as many individual voters as possible face-to-face during the primary season. They schedule hundreds of speeches and appearances all over the country, from sparsely populated rural areas to the nation's largest cities. The candidates appear at rallies and give interviews on television.

In recent years, presidential candidates have begun maintaining Web sites. A citizen can visit the candidate's Web site to find out where he or she is speaking. This is a very good way to follow a candidate's schedule, since a Web site can be updated daily. Any interested person can go to a public event to hear a candidate speak. A person must pay to attend a fundraising event, but the candidates make hundreds of free appearances throughout the campaign.

Debates

During the primary election season, candidates of the same party debate one another. Each candidate is given a set time to respond to questions and to rebut arguments made by opponents. After the national conventions, presidential and vice-presidential candidates of opposing parties may debate one another before the general election.

If a debate is being held in your area, you may be able to attend it. Admission is open to ticket holders. In some debates, candidates take questions directly from voters in the audience.

Only a very limited number of voters can attend debates in person. Since 1960, presidential debates have been broadcast live on television.

Name _____ Date _____

Create a Political Advertisement

    Traditionally, television commercials are the most important tools in a presidential campaign. Campaigns hire high-priced advertising firms to make commercials that will kill the opponent's chances in the election.

    Commercials can make a very strong impression on the voters. Some commercials from years ago are still famous. One 1964 advertisement showed a little girl plucking petals from a daisy while counting "10, 9, 8 . . . ." This image faded out to reveal an atomic testing sight. A nuclear explosion filled the screen when the countdown reached "0." This commercial was considered so shocking that it aired only one time. It was an allusion to Republican Barry Goldwater's support for nuclear weapons. It played on Americans' great fear of nuclear war and helped swing support to the incumbent Democratic president, Lyndon B. Johnson.

Complete the following activity.

    Create a campaign commercial. Work with a group of four to five classmates. Follow these steps:

1. Choose a current prominent politician or a current candidate for president. Your ad can either support or attack this person's candidacy for president.

2. Research your candidate's public record. If you support the candidate, look for strengths. If you are going to create an attack ad, look for weaknesses. Use the Internet and the library to do your research.

3. Pool the results of your research with the members of your group. Discuss which aspect of the candidate's record will make the best subject for your ad.

4. Put your ad together. Write the script and plan the visuals. Each member of the group should contribute ideas to the script.

5. If possible, film your ad. If you don't have the equipment to film, then submit your script instead. The script should include clear descriptions of the visuals you would show on camera.

6. Show your film to the class, or share your script. Discuss which ads were the most effective and why.

Name _____ Date _____

Create a Campaign Theme

A successful presidential campaign is often remembered for a central idea or issue that it focused on. For example, the 1992 Clinton campaign had a sign on the wall of every state headquarters that read, "It's the economy, stupid!" Governor Bill Clinton and his campaign staff realized how worried ordinary Americans were about the economy. Clinton repeatedly promised to reduce the national debt, balance the federal budget, and restore equity to the tax system. His focus on this theme helped win him the 1992 election to the presidency.

Assume that you are about to declare your candidacy for president. Your job is to come up with a central campaign theme. Which major national issue will you spend most of your time discussing?

Complete the following activity.

1. For one week, look through issues of one or more major national newspapers or their Web sites. Sample different television and radio newscasts during this week. Talk to adults of voting age whom you know well and find out about their concerns for the nation. Jot down the major issues that face the United States both at home and abroad.

2. Think about the issue that seems most important to the country. Ask yourself questions such as the following:

    • Which issues are ordinary people concerned about the most?

    • Are people more worried right now about a domestic issue (such as unemployment) or a foreign-policy issue (such as an ongoing war)?

    • How high is the federal deficit? Is there a trade deficit? Is it substantial or minor?

    • Which issues are being covered in the greatest detail by the press?

3. Choose one issue around which you will build your entire campaign. Decide where you stand on this issue and what you can do as president to bring about needed changes and improvements.

4. Write a one-page paper describing your campaign theme. You may want to sum it up in a catchy slogan.

Primary Elections

The word *primary* comes from the Latin *primus,* meaning "first." A **primary election** is like the first round in a sports tournament. Its purpose is to find out quickly which candidate is the favorite among the voters and thus has the best chance of defeating the opposing candidate in the general election.

Each state handles primary elections in its own way. In **open primaries,** citizens can vote for any candidate of any party. In **closed primaries,** citizens must vote with their registered party (i.e., a registered Democrat can vote only for a Democratic candidate).

The direct result of the primary is the assignment of **delegates** to each candidate. These delegates agree to support the candidate to whom they are assigned. The delegates' job is to attend the national party convention and vote on the party's nominee for president.

In some states, the candidate who gets the largest percentage of the popular vote gets all the delegates. In other states, the delegates are divided among the candidates according to the percentage of the popular vote each candidate received.

The political parties determine the number of delegates per state. This number changes from one election year to the next. Larger states get more delegates than smaller ones do. A state that voted heavily in favor of the political party in the last election gets more delegates than a state that favored the opposing party. Republicans and Democrats send thousands of delegates to their national conventions.

Once a candidate has won enough primaries to have the support of the majority of the delegates, he or she is assured of becoming the party nominee. Struggling or losing candidates often withdraw from the race during the primary process. An especially strong contender may be invited to become the vice presidential nominee.

Primaries are not all held on the same day. Instead, they are held over a period of months. Candidates travel to each state in the days and weeks before its primary, campaigning hard for votes. Candidates generally spend more time in larger states that have more delegates.

PRESIDENTIAL TRIVIA

In 1968, Vice President Hubert Humphrey won the Democratic presidential nomination without winning any primaries. In fact, he did not even run in a single primary. Perhaps this is why he lost the general election to Richard Nixon.

Debate the Primary Election Process

You have read that party nominees may be decided before primaries have been held in all the states. This means that all votes are not equal; many will be of no significance at all.

State laws set the date of each primary. New Hampshire's primary is the earliest in the nation. Other states follow in succession. The last primary takes place months after the first one. This means that in any given year, candidates can win enough delegates for the nomination long before the people of many states have even cast their votes.

Your job is to create a primary process that will be fair to the candidates and the voters. Decide on a system that gives each vote as equal a weight as possible without putting an undue campaigning burden on the candidates.

Note that primary elections are not called for in the Constitution. The primary process has evolved over time and is subject to any changes the states care to make.

Complete the following activity.

1. Form a group of five to seven classmates. Sit down together to discuss the primary system.

2. Make sure that everyone understands how the current primary election system works. Discuss people's opinions of the system. Is it equally fair to all voters and to all candidates? Why or why not?

3. Go around the circle and give all members of the group a chance to suggest a system that they think is better than the current one. If anyone thinks the current system is the best possible, have him or her defend that position.

4. Debate and discuss the ideas suggested by the group members. Use these ideas to come to a consensus on a new system for primaries.

5. Share your ideas with the rest of the class. Listen to their conclusions and have a whole-class discussion of how best to reform the system.

Hold a Party Caucus

Some states, such as Iowa and Minnesota, hold a **caucus** instead of a primary election. *Caucus* comes from an Algonquin word meaning roughly "gathering of the tribal chiefs." Registered voters gather at the caucus to choose delegates to the national party conventions. Delegates are not bound to support the candidates favored by the caucus, but they normally follow its preferences. The major difference between a caucus and a primary is that the caucus voters choose candidates openly instead of voting by secret ballot.

Complete the following activity.

Hold a party caucus to decide whom you want to support for president. Follow these steps:

1. Divide the class into two groups. One group will hold a Republican caucus and the other a Democratic caucus.

2. Make a short list of five candidates in your party. Choose among current prominent political figures: senators, representatives, governors, and so on. Include the current president if he or she is eligible to run for a second term.

3. Divide the list of candidates evenly among the members of your caucus. Each student should do some research on his or her candidate. Where does this candidate stand on the major issues of the day? Why would he or she make a good president? Do your research online and/or in the library.

4. Pool your results with the others who were assigned the same candidate. Together, collaborate on a one-page statement that explains why your candidate is the best choice for president. Make copies of your statement and hand them out to everyone in your caucus. Everyone should take one night to read and consider all the statements about all the candidates.

5. Hold the caucus. Vote for your favorite candidate by a show of hands.

   - If a candidate receives at least 15 percent of the vote, he or she gets the support of a proportional share of the state's delegates at the national convention.

   - If a candidate gets less than 15 percent of the vote, he or she is eliminated from the race. People who voted for that candidate must give their support to one of the remaining candidates. The caucus continues until all the voters have agreed to support candidates who have at least 15 percent of the vote. Until all of the losers' supporters have transferred their support to one of the winners, the caucus does not end.

National Conventions

A political convention is a meeting called by a political party. Each party holds its own convention. At these conventions, the parties use **delegates** to decide their leaders and policies. Delegates are representatives of the political party.

Major political parties hold conventions almost every year on the national and state levels. However, the largest conventions take place in the summer of every fourth year, during presidential election years. In these conventions, delegates choose their party's candidate for president.

Before the 1960s, conventions were often the scene of serious fights between different party bosses. In 1924, John W. Davis was nominated after a record 103 ballots at the Democratic National Convention. The Democratic Party was so torn apart by the fight that Republican Calvin Coolidge crushed Davis in the general election.

Conventions like this caused political parties to switch to primary elections to choose candidates. The current Republican and Democratic national conventions have several purposes:

- to make an official announcement of the party nominees

- to rally support for the party nominees

- to write the party platform

- to introduce the candidates to the nation on national television

By the time the national convention is held, the party nominees are already decided. The roll call of delegates at the convention is purely a symbolic ritual.

The **party platform** is the party's political philosophy and its position on the issues. Party leaders meet during the week of the convention and write the platform. Each issue in the platform is called a **plank.** The party platform is not binding in any way on the nominees for president and vice president.

People across the country are already familiar with the candidates. They may have had chances to hear them speak in person during the primary election process. The candidates may have been prominent in public life for a long time. Voters have also had many chances to see advertisements and to read newspaper and Internet articles about the candidates. However, at the national convention the candidate is showcased. He or she has the chance to make a speech of unlimited length, laying out in detail his vision for the nation and what he hopes to accomplish in office.

PRESIDENTIAL TRIVIA

JAMES K. POLK (1795–1849)

A dark horse candidate is a person whose nomination is a surprise. He or she is not well known and was not previously considered a likely candidate. Sometimes a dark horse is selected as a compromise when people cannot decide between candidates that are more famous. The first "dark horse" to become president was James Polk in 1844. He won the Democratic presidential nomination over Martin Van Buren on the eighth ballot. Then he defeated Henry Clay in the general election.

Research a Convention from History

Today, the national nominating conventions are largely a formality. The party nominees have already been decided, and the convention is little more than a rally for the nominee's supporters.

This was not always the case. Throughout U.S. history, there have been many conventions that were titanic battles for power. For example, in 1924, the Democrats took nine days and 103 ballots to choose their nominee and had to call in the police to restore order during a nasty floor fight over the party platform.

Complete the following activity.

Work with a small group of classmates. Choose a national convention from U.S. history and put together an oral/visual presentation for the class. Follow these steps:

1. Choose one of the following national party conventions from history:

> Democratic Convention, 1924
> Republican Convention, 1940
> Democratic Convention, 1948
> Republican Convention, 1964
> Democratic Convention, 1968

2. Find detailed coverage of the convention. Look online and in the library. One good source is the archive of a major newspaper such as the *New York Times.* You might pay special attention to the newspaper of the city where the convention was held (for example, the 1968 Democratic Convention was held in Chicago).

3. Note who the candidates were and what the major issues were. Note who finally won the nomination and how he won it.

4. Plan your presentation. Make sure to include visual elements as well as verbal ones. You might download historic photos from the Internet or use computer software to put together charts showing how the voting went. Use whatever visual elements your audience will find the most interesting and informative.

Polls

The word **poll** is taken from an old Anglo-Saxon word meaning "head." A poll is literally a "head count" of opinions. Organizations take polls to find out where people stand on issues and which candidates they support and why.

Pollsters generally ask two types of questions:

- multiple-choice questions
- questions that must be answered "yes," "no," or "no opinion"

A typical multiple-choice question in a poll will ask you to state your opinion of a particular candidate as "extremely positive," "positive," "negative," or "extremely negative." Sometimes "neutral" or "no opinion" is a fifth option.

The reason for these types of questions is that lengthy or one-of-a-kind answers would take too long for the pollsters to process and would require too much interpretation on their part. Pollsters gather data in a standardized format so they can quickly tally the answers and do not need to interpret what the answers mean.

When polled, you should always do your best to answer the questions honestly. If you have no opinion on a question, that is a perfectly valid answer. For a poll to be meaningful and useful, it is important to have reliable data.

Pollsters normally contact 1,000 people for each poll. It has been generally agreed that the data from 1,000 answers is **statistically significant.** That means that it accurately reflects the opinions of the entire population, within 3 or 4 percentage points. In other words, if 81 percent of the 1,000 people polled answer "yes" to a certain question, that means that between 78 percent and 85 percent of the total population would respond the same way.

Newspapers and major news organizations conduct polls throughout the election process. Political parties and candidates take their own polls. Some candidates insist that they pay no attention to polls. Others have altered their positions on issues because of poll results.

PRESIDENTIAL TRIVIA

HARRY TRUMAN (1884–1972)

In 1948, the *Chicago Tribune* wanted to be the first newspaper with the presidential election results. The editor decided to believe the polls that predicted an easy victory for Thomas Dewey. The newspaper put out an early edition with a huge headline declaring, "Dewey Beats Truman." Only it turned out not to be true. In fact, Harry Truman defeated Dewey rather easily. The pollsters had stopped taking polls two weeks before the election. No one considered the possibility of a last-minute surge by Truman. In addition, the polls were taken by telephone. However, in 1948, people who could afford telephones tended to vote for Dewey. People who could not afford telephones tended to vote for Truman. Of course, these people had no chance to respond to the polls.

Name _____ Date _____

Conduct a Poll

Conduct a poll in your school. Follow these steps:

1. The goal of this poll is to find out which current issue or issues are of the greatest concern to students and whom students would vote for in the upcoming presidential election if it were held immediately.

2. Work with a group of three or four classmates.

3. Write a short list of questions for your poll. Remember that the questions should be answered in one of two ways:

   - "yes," "no," or "no opinion"
   - multiple-choice

   Questions should ask about the two topics listed in Step 1.

   Be careful to phrase your questions so that you don't slant them to make one answer look more favorable or more obvious than another.

   Examples:

Slanted Question	"Please answer *yes, no,* or *no opinion.* Do you want liberal Democrats taking over Congress?"

   This question is unfair because it plays on the negative bias that many people (including some Democrats) feel when they hear the word *liberal.*

Neutral Question	"Please fill in the blank: I would prefer to see the _____ party have the majority in Congress."

   This question is fair because it does not show bias against any party or any political philosophy.

4. Find a time and a place to poll students. One easy method is to print up the questions on a sheet of paper, copy them, and distribute them school-wide, asking students to drop off completed questionnaires the following day.

5. Tabulate the results. Remember that 1,000 people are considered a statistically significant sample of the entire U.S. population; therefore, you need not worry if some students fail to hand in the questionnaire.

6. Announce the results of the poll to the school.

Name _____ Date _____

When Polls Go Wrong

☆★☆

     Polls are an important part of any political campaign in the United States. A poll is a survey of people's opinion. A small group of people, known as a sample, are asked questions by a pollster. The answers of this sample are counted and made public. The answers are supposed to accurately represent the opinions of the larger group. In 1948, Harry Truman ran against Thomas Dewey for president. The polls were taken by telephone. However, at that time, people who could afford telephones tended to vote for Dewey. People who could not afford telephones tended to vote for Truman. Of course, these people had no chance to respond to the polls. The cartoon below is about the election of 1948. It was drawn by Clifford Berryman.

Study the cartoon and answer the questions.

Source: National Archives and Records Administration—Published October 19, 1948

1. Who are the two men in the cartoon? _____

2. What is the significance of the notices on the bulletin board? _____

3. Why do the notices stress how many states the candidate will get? _____

4. Why does Thomas Dewey say "What's the use of going through with the election?"

_____

5. What was the outcome of the election? _____

6. In elections in the United States, polls are used extensively. Do you feel that they are valid? Why or why not?

_____

_____

Cast Your Vote HS, SV 9781419036378

Election Day

On Election Day, **polling places** are usually open from 6:00 A.M. or 7:00 A.M. to 7:00 P.M. or 8:00 P.M. This system ensures that everyone should have a chance to vote either before or after work or school. Voters can walk up to the polling place at any time during these hours. Your polling place is usually a short distance from your residence. It may be a fire station, a school, a library, or even a church.

Volunteers staff polling places, making sure that only people who are properly registered can cast their votes. A volunteer will ask you which **ward** or **precinct** you live in. If you don't know, the volunteer can identify your ward by your street address.

Each ward has a book listing registered voters and their signatures. In most states, you simply sign your name in the book, and the volunteer makes certain that your signature matches. Then you are allowed to cast your vote. Some states have tried to pass laws requiring that voters show photo identification, but these laws have been overturned.

You are guaranteed the opportunity to vote in private. This ensures that no one can pressure you to vote for a certain candidate, and no one can attack you for voting a certain way afterward.

The types of **ballots** used vary. Some are paper cards that you mark with a pen. Others have circles that you must punch out to show your vote. In many locations, people use voting machines. If you have any trouble figuring out how to cast your vote, volunteers will help you.

On your way out, you may be asked to fill out a questionnaire about your voting choices. Your answers are anonymous. The press uses the results of these **exit polls** to predict the election results. After the election is over, the press and both parties analyze the exit-poll data. This data helps candidates understand why they won or lost the election, which issues concern citizens the most, and how to plan for a victory in the next election.

PRESIDENTIAL TRIVIA

When Maine became a state in 1820, it held its elections in September. Maine officials claimed that bad weather, poor roads, and a scattered population made it easier to vote in September than in November. Because Maine held its elections early, the results there were often used to predict the outcome of national elections in November. People began to say, "As Maine goes, so goes the nation." This theory lasted until the presidential election of 1936. In that year, Maine voters in September chose Alf Landon for president. In November, however, only Vermont joined Maine. Landon won only eight electoral votes, and Franklin Roosevelt won one of the greatest landslide victories in U.S. history. No one believed the phrase after that time. In 1957, Maine changed its election law to hold all general elections in November.

Sample Ballots

All images courtesy Computer Electron Systems

The ballot box has long been used and is still a part of voting in fraternal and social organizations for election of officers. White and black marbles were placed in the supply hopper, and the elector would drop one or the other in the voting compartment. "White balls elect and black balls reject" is an old adage in voting by this method. By set rules in the organization, a candidate, good or bad, could be easily "blackballed" by one or two dark spheres appearing in the ballot drawer.

The 1876 Davy vote counting device was basic in design and operation since the voter was merely given the number of balls for each office voted. In a private booth, the voter would drop a ball in the hole under the candidate's name. Voters became aware of the weakness in this method and could drop all three balls in one candidate's box, thereby giving him an advantage over other office seekers. This led to the use of colored marbles, the color to match the particular office voted only, and non-matched colored spheres in the drawer were not counted. The device was nicknamed "Davy's Bird House," after the inventor, Edward Davy.

In this voting booth, electors cast their votes by pulling a lever to record their choices.

In the punch card method, voters were given a ballot card to insert into the vote recorder.

Voters then used a punch stylus to push down through the card for each candidate of choice.

After voting, voters removed the card from the vote recorder and placed it in the ballot envelope.

Official Ballot 1960

☆☆☆☆☆☆☆☆☆☆☆☆☆☆☆☆☆☆☆☆☆☆☆☆☆☆☆☆☆☆☆

In 1960, most Americans voted by marking a paper ballot with a pencil. This is part of the Massachusetts Election Ballot used on November 8, 1960.

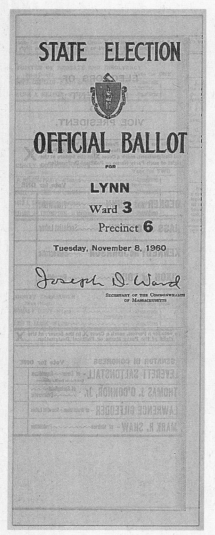

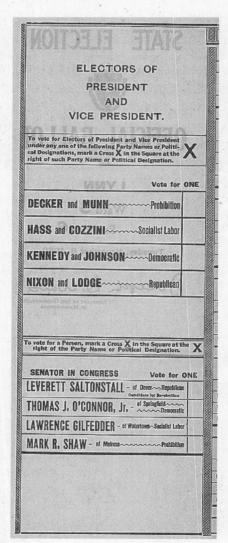

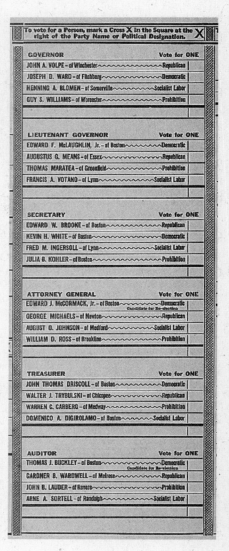

Source: National Archives and Records Administration

Name _____ Date _____

Research Types of Ballots

Ballot designs have changed over time.

For over 100 years, candidates were listed on separate ballots. To vote for your candidate, you had to turn in a ballot with his name printed on it. Only after the Civil War did all candidates of all parties appear on the same ballot.

For many years, ballots included portraits of the major candidates or symbols of the political parties. This made it possible for a voter who could not read to make sure he chose the candidate or party he wanted to support.

In 1960, most Americans still voted by marking a paper ballot with a pencil. Party symbols and all other graphics had disappeared from the ballots by this time.

In recent years, more and more districts have begun to use voting machines. Some machines use a "gear and lever" device. To vote, you push the lever down above the candidate's name. Other machines use punch cards where the voter punches a card inserted behind the printed ballot to record his or her vote.

Today, voting machines use touch screens to record votes. Other computer systems are being developed. Security is always an issue with any voting device.

Complete the following activity.

1. Research the types of voting machines and ballots used in your district. List them below.

   _____

   _____

   _____

2. Research other types of voting machines used elsewhere. List them below.

   _____

   _____

   _____

3. Research new voting devices being developed. List them below.

   _____

   _____

   _____

4. Research the pros and cons of the different types of voting machines used in the past and currently being developed for the future. Consider the problems that were encountered in the 2004 election and ways to address those issues. List your findings on a separate sheet of paper.

5. Compile your results into a report.

Election Day
Cast Your Vote HS, SV 9781419036378

Design a Ballot

Ballots are the actual pieces of paper on which your votes are recorded. The form of ballot varies from one district to the next. Across the nation, there are a great many types of ballots in use.

Many voters have complained that ballots are confusing. During a statewide recount after the 2000 presidential election, thousands of Florida ballots turned out to have been improperly marked. It was generally agreed that these ballots were poorly designed and hard to understand.

If you vote electronically, there may be no ballot at all. Some voting machines simply print out a tally at the end of the day, stating the number of votes cast for each candidate. No paper record is made of individual votes. This means that in close votes, a recount would be very difficult. In the 2004 elections, some voters reported that the voting machines failed to work properly.

Complete the following activity.

Suppose that federal legislation has been passed stating that ballots across the nation will all be the same. Your job is to design a ballot that is fair and easy to use. You may want to look at the ballots on pages 55 and 56 for ideas. Ask yourself these questions:

- Is the ballot easy to read? Are the alternatives clear?

- Should the ballot be available in more than one language?

- Does the person have to mark the ballot with a pen or pencil, or punch holes in it?

- Will the ballot be read by people or by machines?

- Do you see any ambiguities in your ballot design that you can clarify?

- Does your ballot design prevent obvious opportunities for voter fraud?

- Does your ballot prove to the individual voter that he or she has voted as he or she intended to?

- Does your ballot represent all candidates fairly without any preference for party?

Share your ballot designs with the class. Compare and contrast the various designs and evaluate their positive and negative features. Hold a class vote to decide which ballot design is the best.

Name _____   Date _____

The Electoral College

When you cast your vote for president and vice president, you have actually voted for a group of **electors** who are pledged to support those candidates. Each state has two slates of electors, one representing each of the two major parties. Electors are not elected by the people; they are appointed by the political parties. Some of them may have served as delegates to the national convention. The Constitution does not specify any qualifications for electors. Their names are not made public.

The framers of the Constitution created the **Electoral College** because they did not believe that voters were wise enough to choose all of their leaders directly. In the Electoral College system, each state appoints a group of electors equal to the number of that state's senators and representatives combined. This is each state's number of **electoral votes.** The smallest number of electoral votes a candidate needs to win the presidency is 270 (half of the total plus 1). Although Washington, D.C., does not have voting members of Congress, it does have 3 electoral votes. Puerto Rico, American Samoa, and Guam have no electoral votes.

A state's electoral votes are not assigned in proportion to the popular vote. Instead, there is a winner-take-all system. The candidate who gets the highest percentage of the popular vote in any given state gets all its electoral votes. This is how a candidate can lose the popular vote and still win the election.

The electoral ballots are read in Congress in the presence of the full House and Senate. This generally takes place in December. Occasionally through history, an elector has not voted for the candidate to whom he or she was pledged, but this is very rare.

PRESIDENTIAL TRIVIA

Several presidential candidates have won the popular vote but lost in the Electoral College due to the winner-take-all system. These candidates include Andrew Jackson (1824), Samuel Tilden (1876), Grover Cleveland (1888), and Al Gore (2000). Jackson ran for election again and went on to serve two terms in the White House. Cleveland was the incumbent president in 1888. After one term out of office, he ran and won again in 1892. Cleveland is the only person to serve nonconsecutive terms in the White House.

Electoral Votes, 2004

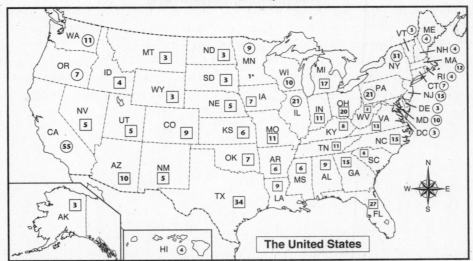

Electoral votes for John Kerry are in circles. ①
Electoral votes for George W. Bush are in squares. ☐1
One electoral vote in Minnesota was cast for John Edwards.

Debate the Electoral College System

Many Americans believe that the Electoral College system is undemocratic and flawed. The issue becomes central to debate every time a presidential candidate loses the popular vote but wins the presidency, which occurred most recently in 2000. When this happens, many people are reminded that the president is not directly elected by the voters. Because of this, some voters call for reform.

Complete the following activity.

Suppose that you are on a Congressional committee to debate whether the system should be reformed. Follow these steps:

1. Work with a group of five to seven classmates.

2. Read Article II and the Twelfth Amendment of the Constitution so that you know exactly how the Electoral College functions. Remember that any change to the Electoral College can be made only by amending the Constitution. Therefore, it must be taken very seriously.

3. Look at the popular vote of the 2000 election. This information should be readily available online or in a recent issue of a world almanac. You can find a breakdown of the popular vote by state.

4. Discuss your impressions of how the Electoral College works. Consider the following questions:

   - Do you believe the Electoral College system is fair to the people?

   - Does it ensure that everyone's vote is counted equally?

   - Has it worked well or poorly throughout history?

   - If you believe the system is flawed, what changes would improve it?

   - If you believe it is the best possible system, on what grounds do you base that opinion?

5. Take a vote on whether your committee would recommend changing the system or keeping it. If you agree that it should be changed, then agree on a new system. Consider whether your new system would be likely to be ratified as a Constitutional amendment.

6. Present the results of the committee's debate to the class. The class then takes on the role of Congress and has an open floor debate about the committee's recommendations.

Name _____ Date _____

Conduct an Election

   Now that you have studied all the steps involved in running for office, you will carry them out. Your job is to conduct an election for a student representative who will work as a liaison between the students and the local police department.

   Large teenage populations cause special concerns for the authorities. Teenagers are old enough to have some freedom and responsibility, but they are too young to be allowed the same freedoms as adults. Teenagers can be easy targets for crime because they are less experienced and more vulnerable than adults.

   In some cities, police have begun reaching out to teens in an effort to get their point of view on the best ways to solve social problems. High schools across the country have student representatives who work directly with police officers.

   Your job is to conduct an election for a student representative/liaison to the local police department. Between candidates' announcements and Election Day, you should allow about two weeks. There are many roles to play in conducting an election.

The Candidates

1. The first thing a candidate for office needs to do is set a purpose for running. Consider the issues involved in being the student liaison to the police. You should know your position on such issues as teen curfews, teen drug use, the necessity for student photo ID cards, and so on.

2. Prepare a brief announcement of your candidacy. Make a concise statement of why you are running for liaison and how you can benefit the student body by filling the position.

3. Write and deliver at least one speech to the student body. Agree to debate the other candidates.

4. Work closely with your campaign staff (see following information) on all aspects of the campaign. Allow your staff to have input on statements and speeches you make. In turn, give them your input on such items as poster and flyer designs and scheduling.

5. Give at least one interview to a reporter (see following information). Be prepared to answer questions from student voters at any time.

Name _____ Date _____

Conduct an Election, continued

The Campaign Manager and Staff

1. Each candidate should have a campaign manager who will take charge of scheduling and planning events. The campaign manager should also design and hang posters, copy and pass out flyers, and stir up support among the student voters. The campaign staff should help the campaign manager with all of these tasks.

2. Campaign staff should regularly sit down with the candidate and discuss strategy. The staff should always be free to give their input on the candidate's speeches and statements. The staff should remember, however, that the candidate is the one in charge of the overall campaign and has the final say.

The Press

1. The press is of great importance in the electoral process. The press informs the ordinary voters about the candidates. It covers their statements, analyzes their ideas, and gives out information about their schedules. Voters depend on the press to learn about the candidates.

2. Each student reporter should conduct a one-on-one interview with each candidate. (If there are too many candidates to make this possible, each reporter can follow one or two candidates closely.) Reporters should only ask questions that have a direct bearing on how the candidate will carry out the duties of the office.

3. Reporters should attend any appearances the candidates make where they are giving speeches or holding debates. Reporters should write articles throughout the campaign. Some articles should simply cover the facts. Others should analyze the campaign and express opinions about which candidate is the best for the job. Articles can be posted online or in the classroom and/or published in the school newspaper.

The Voters

The voters have the important job of paying close attention to the candidates and the issues. Voters should study the issues, such as teen curfews, and decide how they feel about them. They should attend as many appearances by the candidates as their schedules permit. Voters should discuss the candidates among themselves. They should also approach candidates directly with questions or concerns. Their most important responsibility, of course, is to cast their vote on Election Day.

Name _____   Date _____

Conduct an Election, continued

The "State Government"

1. Setting up real elections is the duty of the state. Setting up this school election will be the duty of a group of students who represent "the state." These students should take no active part in any other aspect of the campaign. They should openly express no preference for any of the candidates.

2. This group of students should agree on the date of the election. They will have to get the school's permission to hold the election. They will have to arrange the time and the place within the school where the votes will be cast. They will be in charge of designing and manufacturing the ballots and counting the votes at the end of the day.

3. Students running the election are voters, too. They should pay close attention to the candidates and choose whom to support. However, these students should keep any opinions about the election to themselves. This will help ensure that the election is carried out in a manner that is fair to all the candidates.

Election Day

On the day of the election, follow these steps:

1. Students who are running the election must be prepared with enough ballots and ballot boxes. They must have the polling place or places set up in plenty of time for the election to begin.

2. Voters can walk up to the polling place at any time during its hours to cast their votes. Each voter must be guaranteed the opportunity to vote in secret.

3. The students running the election will count the votes after the polling place closes. If the totals are very close, the votes should be counted a second time. The students should then make an official announcement of the number of votes each candidate received.

4. Whichever candidate has the highest number of votes wins the election. The candidate with the next highest total will be the alternate representative/liaison. The winning candidate may choose to make a victory speech.

Follow an Election

Elections are held throughout the United States in even-numbered years. Every two years, voters go to the polls to elect governors, senators, representatives, mayors, and local officials. Every four years, voters choose a president and vice president as well.

Your job is to play the role of a reporter as you follow the course of an election through all of its stages: the candidates' declarations, the campaigns, and Election Day. If this is a presidential election year, you will also cover the primaries and the national conventions. Throughout the year, you will write a series of articles on what you read, hear, and observe. Your articles will be a mix of factual reporting and analysis.

Since there are several candidates up for election in most years, you should work with a group of people. Together, you represent the staff of the front-page section of a newspaper. You should sit down with your fellow reporters on a weekly basis and discuss the election news of the week. You can also use this time to discuss articles anyone wants to write and ideas people have for interview questions. You can exchange drafts of articles for one another's comments and questions. Putting together a paper is a collaborative process.

At times during the election year, you will want to interview people. Always explain politely that you are writing articles for a project. Many people will be happy to talk to you. Don't persist if people refuse to speak or if they are clearly too busy. Instead, find someone else who can answer your questions.

Follow these steps. Note that some apply only to presidential elections. You will skip these steps if you are covering a midterm election.

Early Stages

1. The election will take place the day after the first Monday in November. If you will be 18 or older by Election Day, register to vote. You can get a copy of your state's voter registration form at a local post office or library, or download it from the Internet. Simply enter the phrase "{name of state} voter registration form" into a search engine. (Residents of North Dakota are not required to register.)

2. Write down the names of the candidates for office. Make a chart showing which candidates represent which political party.

Office	Candidate	Political Party

Follow an Election, continued

3. Go online or to the library to find out what the candidates have said about why they are running for office and what they hope to accomplish. Write an article comparing and contrasting the candidates. You may want to evaluate their statements and their chances based on what you already know about them.

Presidential Elections: The Primaries

4. Each primary election receives extensive coverage in the news media. Follow all the candidates through the primaries. Write articles on these dates:

   - after the New Hampshire primary and Iowa caucuses

   - after "Super Tuesday," on which several states hold primaries at once

   - midway through the primary season, after the New York primary

   - as soon as any candidate clinches a nomination from his or her party

   Report the facts, such as who won and who lost, and how many delegates each candidate received. Analyze any statements the candidates make.

5. Find out where the local campaign headquarters are and pay a visit. Ask someone to show you around the office and explain what the volunteers are doing. Try to interview at least two people. Write an article about the campaign headquarters.

6. If at all possible, find an opportunity to see the candidates in person. Presidential candidates normally establish Web sites on which their schedules of appearances are posted. Your best chance to see the candidates may be right before your state's primary election. Write articles describing any events you attend. If there are several appearances by several candidates, each reporter in your group can attend a different event.

Clinching the Nomination

7. One candidate of each major party generally emerges as the favorite during the primary process. Other candidates may drop out of the race along the way, when they believe they have no chance to win the nomination. When a candidate withdraws from the race, write a short article charting his or her course up to that point. Use your knowledge of the candidate to speculate on his or her political future. Might the candidate be successful in a future election? If he or she is a candidate for president, might he or she become the vice-presidential nominee?

8. If a candidate clinches his or her party's nomination during the primary process, write an article describing the candidate's reaction.

Follow an Election, continued

Presidential Elections: The Nominating Conventions

9. Get together with your group members to watch television coverage of the national party conventions. Broadcast schedules for the conventions are available in advance and can also be found online. Discuss your reactions and then collaborate on a series of articles describing each day of the convention.

The Final Stage of the Campaign

10. Once the conventions are over, the nominees will continue to campaign around the nation. See them in person if possible. If they do not come to your area, you can follow their campaigns in the news media. If the nominees debate one another, write an article on the debates. Assess the candidates' performances.

11. Interview adults of voting age that you know well. Remember that anyone age 18 or older can vote. Ask questions such as the following:

    • Do you intend to vote in the election? If not, why not?

    • Which candidate do you support? Why?

    • Are you volunteering any time to the campaign? If so, please describe your activities.

    Try to interview ten people. Aim for some diversity in the people you interview: they should be of different ages, both male and female, and from different political parties. Write an article describing the trends of their answers and what you believe their answers indicate about the outcome of the general election.

12. Discuss your impressions of the nominees with your fellow reporters. Write an editorial endorsing your choice of the better major-party candidate for the various offices: president, senator, representative, governor, and so on. Remember to back up your endorsement with the facts and evidence that you have gathered during the campaign.

    When a paper endorses a candidate, it is expressing the view of its editorial staff, not just one person. This means that the staff members discussed the article together and accept joint credit for its authorship. You should therefore collaborate on your editorial.

    If the group cannot reach a consensus on which is the better candidate for president, you may divide into two small groups and write two editorials, one endorsing each candidate.

Follow an Election, continued

Election Day

13. In the afternoon, go to your polling place and cast your vote. Don't go too early in the day, because you will want to ask questions once you are there.

   If volunteers are collecting exit-poll data, ask one of them for an interview. Ask whether the volunteer can tell you anything about the results of the exit polls, or if he or she has any idea how the voting is proceeding. Ask if the turnout has been heavy or light.

   Write an article describing your experience of voting. Was the ballot easy to understand? Was anyone denied the opportunity to vote? Did the voting machines seem to be working properly? If you and your fellow reporters voted at different polling places, compare your experiences. You may want to work together on a joint article.

14. On election night, watch the returns with your fellow reporters. You can follow returns online or on television. Reporters will announce results as early as possible. You should begin watching at 9:00 P.M. Eastern Standard Time. Since polls on the East Coast are usually open until 8:00 P.M., meaningful results are not likely until 9:00.

15. Work together on an article describing the most interesting results of the elections. Consider the following questions:

   • Did the current minority party win control of the House and/or the Senate? Will the new president have a majority supporting him or her in Congress?

   • Were any of the elections considered "upset" victories? If so, which ones?

Voter Registration Form

☆☆☆☆☆☆☆☆☆☆☆☆☆☆☆☆☆☆☆☆☆☆☆☆☆☆☆☆

In 49 of the 50 states, citizens must register to vote. (North Dakota does not require voter registration.) To register, you must fill out a form.

The form below is a national voter registration form. To register, fill the form out and mail it to the address provided by your home state. There are three states that do not use this form:

- New Hampshire accepts this form only as an application for a New Hampshire mail-in voter registration form.
- North Dakota does not register its voters.
- Wyoming state law prohibits acceptance of this form.

Go online to find your state's voter registration form. Type "{name of state} voter registration form" into a search engine. Download and print the form and compare it to the one below. Each state has a slightly different from, but they all ask for basically the same information.

Federal law requires that all voters must be U.S. citizens at least 18 years of age. Each state has a different residency requirement.

Voter Registration Application
Before completing this form, review the General, Application, and State specific instructions.

Are you a citizen of the United States of America? ☐ Yes ☐ No Will you be 18 years old on or before election day? ☐ Yes ☐ No **If you checked "No" in response to either of these questions, do not complete form.** (Please see state-specific instructions for rules regarding eligibility to register prior to age 18.)		This space for office use only.

#				
1	(Circle one) Mr. Mrs. Miss Ms.	Last Name	First Name	Middle Name(s)	(Circle one) Jr Sr II III IV
2	Home Address		Apt. or Lot #	City/Town	State	Zip Code
3	Address Where You Get Your Mail If Different From Above			City/Town	State	Zip Code
4	Date of Birth ___/___/___ Month Day Year	**5**	Telephone Number (optional)	**6**	ID Number - (See Item 6 in the instructions for your state)
7	Choice of Party (see item 7 in the instructions for your State)	**8**	Race or Ethnic Group (see item 8 in the instructions for your State)		

#		
9	I have reviewed my state's instructions and I swear/affirm that: ■ I am a United States citizen ■ I meet the eligibility requirements of my state and subscribe to any oath required. ■ The information I have provided is true to the best of my knowledge under penalty of perjury. If I have provided false information, I may be fined, imprisoned, or (if not a U.S. citizen) deported from or refused entry to the United States.	Please sign full name (or put mark) ▲ Date: ___ ___/___/___ Month Day Year

If you are registering to vote for the first time: please refer to the application instructions for information on submitting copies of valid identification documents with this form.

68

Name _____ Date _____

Presidents and Vice Presidents of the United States

1 **George Washington (1789–1797)**
V.P. John Adams (1789–1797)

2 **John Adams (1797–1801)**
V.P. Thomas Jefferson (1797–1801)

3 **Thomas Jefferson (1801–1809)**
V.P. Aaron Burr (1801–1805)
V.P. George Clinton (1805–1809)

4 **James Madison (1809–1817)**
V.P. George Clinton (1809–1812)
V.P. Elbridge Gerry (1813–1814)

5 **James Monroe (1817–1825)**
V.P. Daniel Tompkins (1817–1825)

6 **John Quincy Adams (1825–1829)**
V.P. John C. Calhoun (1825–1829)

7 **Andrew Jackson (1829–1837)**
V.P. John C. Calhoun (1829–1832)
V.P. Martin Van Buren (1833–1837)

8 **Martin Van Buren (1837–1841)**
V.P. Richard M. Johnson (1837–1841)

9 **William Henry Harrison (1841)**
V.P. John Tyler (1841)

10 **John Tyler (1841–1845)**
No vice president

11 **James K. Polk (1845–1849)**
V.P. George M. Dallas (1845–1849)

12 **Zachary Taylor (1849–1850)**
V.P. Millard Fillmore (1849–1850)

13 **Millard Fillmore (1850–1853)**
No vice president

14 **Franklin Pierce (1853–1857)**
V.P. William R. King (1853)

15 **James Buchanan (1857–1861)**
V.P. John C. Breckenridge (1857–1861)

16 **Abraham Lincoln (1861–1865)**
V.P. Hannibal Hamlin (1861–1865)
V.P. Andrew Johnson (1865)

17 **Andrew Johnson (1865–1869)**
No vice president

18 **Ulysses S. Grant (1869–1877)**
V.P. Schuyler Colfax (1869–1873)
V.P. Henry Wilson (1873–1875)

19 **Rutherford B. Hayes (1877–1881)**
V.P. William A. Wheeler (1877–1881)

20 **James A. Garfield (1881)**
V.P. Chester A. Arthur (1881)

21 **Chester A. Arthur (1881–1885)**
No vice president

22 **Grover Cleveland (1885–1889)**
V.P. Thomas A. Hendricks (1885)

23 **Benjamin Harrison (1889–1893)**
V.P. Levi P. Morton (1889–1893)

24 **Grover Cleveland (1893–1897)**
V.P. Adlai E. Stevenson (1893–1897)

25 **William McKinley (1897–1901)**
V.P. Garret A. Hobart (1897–1899)
V.P. Theodore Roosevelt (1901)

26 **Theodore Roosevelt (1901–1909)**
V.P. Charles W. Fairbanks (1905–1909)

27 **William Howard Taft (1909–1913)**
V.P. James S. Sherman (1909–1912)

28 **Woodrow Wilson (1913–1921)**
V.P. Thomas R. Marshall (1913–1921)

29 **Warren G. Harding (1921–1923)**
V.P. Calvin Coolidge (1921–1923)

30 **Calvin Coolidge (1923–1929)**
V.P. Charles G. Dawes (1925–1929)

31 **Herbert Hoover (1929–1933)**
V.P. Charles Curtis (1929–1933)

32 **Franklin D. Roosevelt (1933–1945)**
V.P. John Nance Garner (1933–1941)
V.P. Henry A. Wallace (1941–1945)
V.P. Harry S. Truman (1945)

32 **Harry S. Truman (1945–1953)**
V.P. Alben W. Barkley (1949–1953)

33 **Dwight D. Eisenhower (1953–1961)**
V.P. Richard M. Nixon (1953–1961)

34 **John F. Kennedy (1961–1963)**
V.P. Lyndon B. Johnson (1961–1963)

35 **Lyndon B. Johnson (1963–1969)**
V.P. Hubert H. Humphrey (1965–1969)

36 **Richard M. Nixon (1969–1974)**
V.P. Spiro T. Agnew (1969–1973)
V.P. Gerald R. Ford (1973–1974)

37 **Gerald R. Ford (1974–1977)**
V.P. Nelson A. Rockefeller (1974–1977)

38 **James Carter (1977–1981)**
V.P. Walter F. Mondale (1977–1981)

39 **Ronald Reagan (1981–1989)**
V.P. George H. Bush (1981–1989)

40 **George H. Bush (1989–1993)**
V.P. J. Danforth Quayle (1989–1993)

41 **William Clinton (1993–2001)**
V.P. Albert Gore Jr. (1993–2001)

42 **George W. Bush (2001–   )**
V.P. Richard B. Cheney (2001–   )

Presidents and Vice Presidents
Cast Your Vote HS, SV 9781419036378

Name _____ Date _____

The Election Process

☆☆☆☆☆☆☆☆☆☆☆☆☆☆☆☆☆☆☆☆☆☆☆☆☆☆☆☆☆☆☆☆☆☆

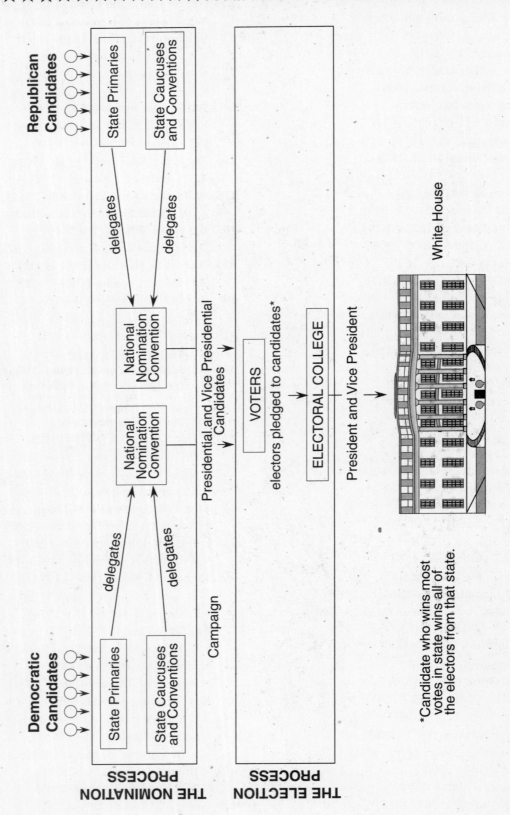

Republican Candidates

State Primaries

State Caucuses and Conventions

delegates

delegates

National Nomination Convention

Democratic Candidates

State Primaries

State Caucuses and Conventions

delegates

delegates

National Nomination Convention

Campaign

Presidential and Vice Presidential Candidates

VOTERS

electors pledged to candidates*

ELECTORAL COLLEGE

President and Vice President

White House

*Candidate who wins most votes in state wins all of the electors from that state.

THE NOMINATION PROCESS

THE ELECTION PROCESS

Answer Key

Pages 3–4

1. A	11. A
2. C	12. C
3. B	13. B
4. D	14. B
5. D	15. B
6. B	16. A
7. C	17. B
8. C	18. D
9. D	19. B
10. C	20. C

Page 7

Typical reasons for not voting: too busy, things never change no matter who is in power, all politicians are corrupt and dishonest, I don't like my choices, this is only a local election so it isn't important. Typical reasons for believing in the importance of voting: it is our responsibility as citizens; it is our chance to have some say in who our leaders are; it is our chance to force a bad or incompetent leader out of office. Make sure students provide reasonable, well-supported arguments.

Page 9

Make sure that all students participate. Monitor students as they plan and carry out the vote. Help them as needed with each step. Make sure they have found an issue of sufficient interest and importance on which most of the school population will want to vote.

Page 12

Answers will vary according to the nation selected. Tell students that they can find many of these answers in the most recent issue of a world almanac or in recent encyclopedia articles. You might advise them against using Wikipedia.com since anyone can post anything they want to on Wikipedia. Check students' work to be sure that they have answered the questions accurately.

Page 15

1. executive, legislative, and judicial
2. They did not want any one branch of the government to have too much power.
3. to make laws, to confirm or reject presidential appointments and international treaties, to give consent to going to war
4. judicial
5. The president appoints Supreme Court justices. The president can veto any bill Congress wants to make law.
6. the Senate and the House of Representatives
7. They can vote leaders into and out of office.
8. The Supreme Court can overturn any law passed by Congress and the president by deciding the law is unconstitutional.
9. A majority of both houses of Congress must vote in favor of the bill. It is then sent to the president for his or her signature. If the president signs the bill, it becomes a law.
10. Members of the two parties generally oppose one another. Members of each party must debate, persuade, and argue to win support from the other party. If the president is of one party and the majority of members of Congress are of the opposing party, this becomes an obstacle to passing legislation.

Page 16

1. May 18, 1948
2. Congress and President Harry Truman
3. the separation of powers between the three branches of government, specifically here between the executive branch and the legislative branch

4. Congress is moving into the area of the president's authority.
5. to keep one branch of government from becoming too powerful

Page 18

Answers will vary depending on the chosen state. Remind students that every state has a home page and that every state's constitution can be found online. Check to be sure that students have answered the questions accurately.

Page 20

Make sure that all group members participate. Guide students through the task of putting the presentation together, as needed. Make sure that they have accurately described the local government in your area.

Page 22

Answers will vary depending on the chosen leader. Make sure that students' essays are organized and state clearly the reasons they admire this leader.

Page 24

Take time to discuss speeches with students during the first draft phase. Encourage them to read past presidents' inaugural addresses. Make sure that their speeches do not run longer than the suggested limit and that they fulfill the proper purposes for an inaugural address.

Page 26

Make sure that all students in the group participate. Make sure that they make reasonable choices of candidates and that they make reasonable, well-supported arguments for the candidates.

Page 28

Reasons Washingtonians should have equal rights and privileges: They are U.S. citizens. The Constitution guarantees all citizens equal representation. Reasons against: Washington is not a state. Only states have the right to two senators and voting representatives. Washingtonians are represented in a general way by all the members of Congress, as are the rest of the nation's citizens. Make sure that students give reasonable, well-supported arguments for their side of the question.

Page 30

1. California is the largest state because it has the greatest number of representatives.
2. The minimum number of representatives is one, and seven states have one representative. The map does not show which of these is the smallest.
3. A candidate can win if he/she carries 11 states. They are:

    CA—55
    TX—34
    NY—31
    FL—27
    IL—21
    PA—21
    OH—20
    MI—17
    NJ—15
    NC—15
    GA—15
    ‾‾‾‾‾
    271

Page 31

1.–4. Answers will vary depending on where students live. The best Internet resources for this information are www.house.gov and the home page of the student's home state. The best print resource is a current world almanac.

5.–6. Answers will vary. Make sure that students have selected issues that are appropriate for a representative in Congress; they should not be too local in their scope.

7. Students can find this information at www.house.gov. They can also telephone the House of Representatives at 1-202-225-3121.

8.–10. Letters will vary. Encourage students to watch for a reply and to share it with the class if they receive one.

Page 32

1. July 28, 1946

2. John Q. Public represents the voters.

3. He is talking about voting for different candidates for Congress than those currently in office.

4. November refers to the time of the election.

5. Check that students give reasonable, well-supported statements of their view.

Page 35

Make sure that all team members participate in the debate.

Page 37

Editorials will vary depending on the issues chosen. Make sure students make reasonable, well-supported arguments.

Page 39

Make sure students have accurately retold the history of the party they chose.

Page 41

Make sure students have written reasonable, well-supported arguments for the candidates of their choice.

Page 44

Meet with each group of students and give them any advice or technical assistance they need. Encourage class discussion of each of the commercials.

Page 45

Make sure students have chosen reasonable, viable campaign themes and made good arguments for basing a campaign on these themes.

Page 47

Make sure that all students participate in the debate and that they support their ideas with reasonable arguments.

Page 48

Meet with each group of students to make sure that the caucuses are carried out in an organized fashion.

Page 50

If applicable, share your own memories of past conventions with students. Encourage them to talk to adults who are old enough to remember these conventions. Give students any guidance they need in finding visual materials for their presentations. Make sure that all students participate.

Page 52

Give students any necessary help in phrasing their poll questions appropriately. Work with students to get necessary permission from school authorities to involve the entire school in participating. You may want to have faculty members involved in counting and tabulating the questionnaires.

Page 53

1. Harry Truman and Thomas Dewey

2. The poll results are posted, giving Dewey the lead by a wide margin.

3. Presidents are elected by the Electoral College, not by individual votes.

4. Dewey considers the poll results an indication of a clear victory.

5. Harry Truman was elected.

6. Check that students give reasonable, well-supported statements of their view.

Page 57

Make sure students' reports are accurate.

Page 58

Examine students' ballots and provide constructive criticism of their designs. Display ballots in the classroom.

Page 60

Make sure that all team members participate and give reasonable, well-supported arguments for their decisions.

Pages 61–63

Give students any help they need in finding a role to play in the election process. Make sure that you have a reasonable number of students in all the categories. Contact the local police department to make the results of the election a reality rather than just an academic exercise. You may want to have faculty members involved in supervising the voting and in counting votes.

Pages 64–67

This activity covers an entire year from November to November. Students who are in your class at the start of the activity may not be yours any longer the following November. Therefore, you should work with the teacher they will have in this subject next year.

Sit down with each group of students at the start of the election cycle. Give them any guidance they need about how to get started. Encourage them to read the newspapers and watch a variety of television broadcasts. These will be good models to follow. Since the election cycle continues through the summer when school is not in session, encourage students to keep up their work. Arrange to meet with them or answer their questions by telephone or e-mail. During the summer, students can post their articles online for others to read.